Anatomy of Professional Practice

Promising Research Perspectives on Educational Leadership

Fenwick W. English

The University of North Carolina at Chapel Hill

D1502103

Rowman & Littlefield Education
Lanham • New York • Toronto • Plymouth, UK

Published in the United States of America
by Rowman & Littlefield Education
A Division of Rowman & Littlefield Publishers, Inc.
A wholly owned subsidary of The Rowman & Littlefield Publishing
Group, Inc.
4501 Forbes Boulevard, Suite 200, Lanham, Maryland 20706
www.rowmaneducation.com

Estover Road
Plymouth PL6 7PY
United Kingdom

British Library Cataloguing in Publication Information Available

Library of Congress Cataloging-in-Publication Data

English, Fenwick W.
  Anatomy of professional practice : promising research perspectives on
educational leadership / Fenwick W. English.
      p. cm.
  ISBN-13: 978-1-57886-673-1 (cloth : alk. paper)
  ISBN-10: 1-57886-673-1 (cloth : alk. paper)
  ISBN-13: 978-1-57886-674-8 (pbk. : alk. paper)
  ISBN-10: 1-57886-674-X (pbk. : alk. paper)
  1. Teachers—Professional relationships—United States. 2. Educational
leadership—United States. 3. Education—Research—United States.
4. Postmodernism and education—United States. I. Title.
  LB1775.2.E53 2008
  371.1—dc22   2007020820

™ The paper used in this publication meets the minimum requirements
of American National Standard for Information Sciences—Permanence of
Paper for Printed Library Materials, ANSI/NISO Z39.48-1992.
Manufactured in the United States of America.

Contents

Foreword

Disciplines develop through critique, debate, and argument. In other words, dissent is not only healthy, it is necessary. Fenwick English acknowledges this dissenter role, one for which he is well adapted. His *Anatomy* is a text that speaks to the core of the discipline, of relevance for scholars, graduate students (heading toward an academic or a practitioner vocation), and practitioners, including government and policy actors, informing research and curricular development in universities and professional development in the field.

This volume is, as Fenwick English acknowledges in his introduction, a line of argument developed over at least a decade of scholarship exploring the legitimate scope and grounding for school leadership practice. And this decade has been fruitful, including many books and articles, most notably *The Postmodern Challenge to the Theory and Practice of Educational Administration* (2003), the forthcoming *Art of Educational Leadership: Balancing Performance and Accountability*, and *The SAGE Handbook of Educational Leadership* (2005) and *The SAGE Encyclopedia of Educational Leadership and Administration* (2006). In some senses this book is a synthesis of many evaluations of the field made during this period. It is certainly a bold and deftly handled approach to the basis of knowledge, ideological influences affecting our acceptance of knowledge, and a persuasive argument for adopting a sensibility rooted in compassion rather than the more prevalent concept of "caring" that is too easily bent to maintaining the status quo and serving bureaucratic ends. What emerges is more than an assemblage of individual arguments, it is a coherent

and encompassing perspective woven together into a Weltanschau-
ung, an understanding to which educational leaders at all levels of
education, including higher education, could aspire.

There are many indications of the maturity of a field. Judging by
other disciplines like political science, sociology, philosophy, aesthetics, and history (all relevant to educational administration and
leadership), these include biographies of its major scholars, histories
of its intellectual movements, and, most importantly, a critique of its
first principles, that is, an examination of its philosophical foundation for knowledge theory, ethics, and ontology, even in a field that
is applied or professional. Public administration has gone through
several "crises" of legitimacy, spawning productive debates and ultimately a more solid and broad foundation upon which to ground
professional practice as well as scholarship. However, educational
administration and leadership have been comparatively less successful in critiquing the state of the discipline. Envisaged here as an
anatomy in the classic meaning of the term, ascertaining the "position, relations, structure, and function" of school leadership, that
makes an important contribution to generating attention to first principles in several domains of scholarship and professionalism.

There are three interdependent sections to the *Anatomy*, all of
which are crafted through a deeply understood use of primary disciplines informing educational administration and leadership, ranging
from the social to the natural sciences. The first is the initial argument of replacing caring with compassion, later picked up in part 9
as a discussion of morality and the means of achieving social justice.
The second presents Dewey's claim that education is more an
artistry than a science of behavior, expanded on in parts 7, 8, and 9
through research activities, leadership practice as a performative art,
and the aesthetic grounding for morality. The final is an examination
of the scientistic ideology dominant in the field that has inhibited not
only the expansion of scholarship and professional development into
many qualitative and humanistic directions but a critique of scien-
tism as an appropriate foundation upon which to build. Parts 3, 4,

and 5 explore this "pseudoscience" adopted all too often in a cursory manner, lacking due attention to the limitations of science and a long twentieth-century history of debate in knowledge theory by such figures as Feyerabend, Lakatos, Popper, Peirce, and Gadamer about the unsuitability of natural science for the study of human experience and accepting all too readily a mythology of the rational practice and formulation of science.

What Fenwick English proposes is educational leadership that is aesthetically and qualitatively grounded and in professional expression an art. It is this kind of foundation that provides access to moral judgment and social justice, knowledge and skill development as something more than routine managerial tasks, and the means to question and overcome ideology. The *Anatomy* is a timely contribution under current economic regimes bent on transforming education into a commercial venture. Its reception will determine whether the perspective presented here will be taken up as an opportunity for growth or whether through ideological resistance it will be relegated to tilting at windmills. I would hope for the health of educational administration and leadership that it is the former that will bear out.

Eugenie Samier
Simon Fraser University, Canada

Introduction: Why an Anatomy?

This book began as the speech for my 2007 Presidential Address for the Annual Meeting of the University Council for Educational Administration (UCEA). It soon expanded beyond a speech into a more full-fledged text. I am extremely grateful for so many conversations over the years with colleagues who took time to consider my ideas and criticisms and offered advice and counsel to me, not to mention friendship and support. It is well known that I am a dissenter to much of the movement toward the kind of educational standards for the preparation of educational leaders that have been enshrined in state exams and accreditation reviews as well as to the kinds of research approaches advocated by such agencies as the National Research Council. Indeed, these criticisms continue in this work.

With that in mind, the "anatomy" in the book title is a deliberate choice. One of the dictionary definitions of anatomy is "the art of separating the parts of an animal or plant in order to ascertain their position, relations, structure, and function" (*Webster's* 1972, 33). Too often, discussions about professional practice are concerned only with standards or research methods or facets of school leadership. One of the purposes of this text is to sketch out an anatomy of professional practice and illustrate how any such discussions are anchored in epistemological claims or assumptions and also that practices are always theory- and ideology-embedded, even if we are ignorant about their presence. Any such discussions that do not acknowledge the presence of these elements are naïve at best or potentially destructive at worst, because they have no sense of the direction or impact on the profession in its longitudinal development.

In this text I call this "the Pasteur problem." Once one begins to recognize that standards themselves are not unproblematic and largely rest on political power rather than on empirical justification, then discussions regarding social justice become even more imperative.

This text contains a line of argument, that is, a perspective or narrative, which has been constructed over a decade, mostly in symposia papers at Divisions A and L of the American Education Research Association, the University Council of Educational Administration, and the National Council of Professors of Education as well as through subsequent publication in refereed journals and book chapters, notably my 2003 text *The Postmodern Challenge to the Theory and Practice of Educational Administration* and the 2008 text *The Art of Educational Leadership: Balancing Performance and Accountability.* I view a line of argument from a postmodern perspective, that is, a centered viewpoint, which itself can be deconstructed in the Derridian tradition of deconstruction. So I am not about constructing a metanarrative to replace the ones I criticize. However, I am not a postmodernist who refuses to take a position. I believe it is incumbent on anyone deconstructing a practice or a theory in an applied profession like ours to have something to offer as an alternative. The difference perhaps is that my proposed alternatives have nowhere near the certitude of the metanarratives I have deconstructed. Certitude is an unwarranted disposition in considering matters of professional practice, especially the practice of educational leadership. I find in the current discourse of standard-setting and accreditation a self-confirming smugness that reeks of false certitude, exactitude, and universality (see Peirce 1955). A little more humility by its proponents as to the temporality of their work and a shade more public recognition of the shortcomings of their standards would certainly be welcome from my perspective. But their silence on such issues is indicative of their lack of concern or their ignorance about such issues. That is even more troubling, given the long history of embedded prejudices that have so long been a part of our discourse.

Although I am a passionate advocate and in many ways an unrepentant romantic, in no way should my emotion be construed as a lack of respect for my colleagues who disagree with me. My opposition to the prevailing thought of the day is not a sign that I doubt their sincerity or integrity. It is rather a sign that the outcome of the conversation and debate continues to be important, because the stakes are enormously high for the future of public education and our profession.

I have been privileged to have lived in a period of great ferment and public turmoil regarding the nature of education in America. I should like to dedicate this text to my father and mother, Melvin and Phyllis English (1910–2001), who as public school teachers in the Los Angeles City Schools included me in their conversations, frustrations, and occasional periods of professional joy as they pursued their careers as classroom teachers in the cause of public education in California.

There were times over the years that the continuing pursuit of public education—as it has been envisioned as a ladder to a better life, a ladder that could be traversed by anyone but whose historical record is nowhere near that ideal—might, could, or should have been abandoned. To this prospect I have demurred. The great brain surgeon Harvey Cushing in his last speech to his colleagues captured my feelings when he quoted the Talmud, "The day is short and work is great. The reward is also great and the Master praises. It is not incumbent on thee to complete the work but thou must not therefore cease from it" (Bliss 2005, 512). Even after all these years, public education is still an experiment and the jury is still out. The ideal is worth fighting for, even as the reality is less than ideal, for none of the proffered alternatives are half as good for healing the divisions in our society and move us toward the true democracy we hope to become.

Fenwick W. English
R. Wendell Eaves Distinguished Professor of Educational Leadership
School of Education
University of North Carolina at Chapel Hill

REFERENCES

Bliss, M. (2005). *Harvey Cushing: A life in surgery.* Oxford: Oxford University Press.

Buchler, J., ed. (1955) *Philosophical Writings of Peirce.* New York: Dover.

Webster's Seventh New Collegiate Dictionary (1972). Springfield, MA: G. & C. Merriam Company.

PART 1

Compassion Is Different from Caring

The word *compassion* is not very often found in the literature of educational leadership/educational administration. It is not found in the Interstate School Leaders Licensure Consortium (ISLLC) standards (see Hessell and Holloway 2002; Shipman, Queen, and Peel 2007), nor is it a word common within the traditional introductory texts that have been widely used in preparation programs (see Cunningham and Cordeiro 2000; Haller and Strike 1986; Hanson 1991; Hoy and Miskel 1982; Lunenburg and Ornstein 1991; Owens 1987; Owens and Valesky 2007). Nor is compassion reflected in the reviews of research conducted in the field (see Boyan 1988; Murphy and Seashore Louis, 1999). And despite some recent texts which center on the notion of *caring* within educational administration, this idea has been advanced as a means to administer schools linked to student outcomes, confronting contemporary social problems, or "rethinking organizational structures" (Beck 1994, 58) instead of dealing with the internal capacity and the commitment to deal with others' distress or oppression, that is, pursuing an agenda of social justice, or what Furman and Shields (2005) and others have called "deep democracy" (121–23).

Perhaps one reason is that compassion, which means "sympathetic consciousness of others' distress together with a desire to alleviate it" (Merriam-Webster 2003, 253), connotes a system of values and a moral outlook that has little to do with the vocabulary of *efficiency* and scientific empiricism (Keeton 1984), which now dominates the field in method and outlook and which has envisioned caring principally as a means of molding communities that support the existing methods and means of schooling (see Beck and Foster 1999, 355).

When caring (or when compassion is synonymous with caring; see Glickman, Gordon, and Ross-Gordon 2007, 452) is employed as a means to extend popular schooling practices such as total quality management (TQM) and "black-box economic models" as embodied in the ISLLC/ELCC (Educational Leadership Constituent Council) standards, then it is a soft form of co-opting resistance to the current isomorphism between institutional structures and larger social hierarchies of power and privilege (see Fazzaro, Walter, and McKerrow 1995, 92; Wiens 2006). I shall argue that compassion is a more radical concept than caring. One can *care* about poor people without doing anything about poverty. I argue that compassion is the wellspring for acting on problems of poverty or social justice.

Perhaps one of the most remarkable and radical leaders who employed compassion as leverage for significant social justice activism was Mahatma Gandhi. R. Iyer commented about the concept of compassion as utilized by Gandhi:

> A genuinely compassionate man (*karunika*) suffers with the sorrow of other beings and thus his ego-centered mind expands, acquiring a wider field of action. In the words of a Buddhist text, "action which is without wisdom is a fetter. Wisdom which cannot be expressed in action is a barren abstraction. Action combined with wisdom is freedom, wisdom combined with action is freedom." (1973, 237)

The nexus of Gandhi's concept of compassion was his devotion to the idea of *ahimsa*. Roughly translated, *ahimsa* means nonviolence (Iyer 1973, 178). But Gandhi transformed the idea of nonviolence into a political agenda by providing it with a negative and a positive interpretation. The negative side was concerned with not causing the destruction of life by deliberate or even unconscious actions. In Gandhi's words, "A votary of ahimsa therefore remains true to his faith if the spring of all his actions is compassion" (1968, 522). But the positive side of *ahimsa* included "the largest love, the greatest charity. . . . This active Ahimsa necessarily includes truth and fearlessness" (Iyer 1973, 180). And for Gandhi *ahimsa* implied "an inability to go on witnessing another's pain and from it thus spring mercy, heroism and all other virtues associated with ahimsa" (Iyer 1973, 182). The positive side of *ahimsa,* centered on compassion, became "a refusal to submit to injustice" (Iyer 1973, 183).

The hard rock of Gandhi's political action agenda involved a profound sense of respect and compassion:

> Ahimsa . . . is the minimal and mandatory demand of human morality. This is justified in terms of the Golden Rule, but also on the basis of the belief in the sanctity and oneness of all life and the identity of interests of all men by virtue of their common dignity and their moral interdependence. Ahimsa [is] the only way in which we can express our respect for the innate worth of any human being. It is an essential and universal obligation without which we would cease to be human. (Iyer 1973, 184)

It also seems to me to be entirely appropriate for an enterprise dealing with children to be stewarded by compassionate leaders. But with the current political and methodological cross-currents of our field, preparing compassionate leaders would be a formidable task. It is to this issue that I would like to turn.

PART 2

Dewey's Differentiation

Figure 1 is based on a view of the landscape of preparation programs from a perspective adopted by John Dewey that "education is a mode of life, of action. As an act it is wider than science" (1929, 75). Dewey (1964/1926) wrote widely on artistic issues. Science is concerned with knowledge and definition. Art, however, is concerned with performance. Dewey puts it this way as it pertains to something like *compassion*:

> Art also explicitly recognizes what it has taken so long to discover in science: the control of re-shaping natural conditions exercised by emotions and the place of the imagination, under the influence of desire in recreating the world into a more orderly place. When so-called non-rational factors are found to play a large part in the production of relations of consistency and order in logical systems, it is not surprising that they should operate in artistic structures. Indeed, it may be questioned whether any scientific systems extant . . . equal artistic structure in integrity, subtlety and scope. (1964/1926, 144)

I want to take this word compassion, which on the surface appears to be an intuitively desirable orientation for educational leadership, to probe the reasons why it is not commonplace among the criteria for educational leadership programs I know today, either in accreditation standards or as an objective of leadership preparation. I will argue that without compassion we cannot become effective leaders for social justice, nor will we be able to advance in any significant way our understanding of leadership or improve its effectiveness beyond the metaphors and models of efficiency which are already regnant in our discourse; to some critics the lack may actually interfere with enabling schools to be more humane and socially just places (see Larson and Murtadha 2002; Shoho, Merchant, and Lugg 2005; Marshall and Oliva 2006).

And while there is a great deal of discussion today about *distributed leadership* (Spillane 2006), I will argue that while schools may not need heroes who are effaced in the concept of distributed leadership (Lakomski 2005), they will always need heroic action, which was Gandhi's perspective. Gandhi eschewed heroes, but he fully embraced the need for heroic actions, and he was mightily influenced by a work we have unfortunately largely trashed for the wrong reasons, Thomas Carlyle's *On Heroes, Hero-Worship, and the Heroic in History* (1841/1935). We have imposed an empirical, largely quantitative lens on Carlyle's treatise and assessed it against what it can tell us empirically about leadership. That was never Carlyle's intent.

> Science has done much for us; but it is a poor science that would hide from us the great deep sacred infinitude of nescience [lack of knowledge, ignorance], whither we can never penetrate, on which all science swims as a mere superficial film. This world, after all our science and sciences, is still a miracle; wonderful, inscrutable, magical and more, to whosoever will think of it. (Carlyle 1841/1935, 10)

I view Carlyle's work as an effort to understand the connection between the inner and outer worlds of leaders. To use Dewey's distinction between science and art, Carlyle was probing what the logic of empiricism would label the "non-rational factors," which can be better understood within the framework of Dewey's "artistic structures" than through the lens of science. Science has destroyed Carlyle as it has so many other playwrights, poets, and painters who have dealt with leadership or the dilemmas of leadership on the broad landscape of connecting human interiorities and contextual externalities (see English 2006a).

In this sense the artist has a much deeper appreciation of the subjectivity of leadership than many of the researchers toiling in the vineyards of educational administration in our times, some of whom have erased any need for leaders at all (see Nielsen 2004; Lakomski 2005). I am impressed with the words of Henri Cartier-Bresson, one of the world's premier photographers, who wrote, "If, in making a portrait, you hope to grasp the interior silence of a willing victim, it's very difficult, but you must somehow position the camera between his shirt and his skin" (2005, 79). This kind of artistic "objectivity" is much different from many of those working the "leadership circuit" in research today. In too many cases I see no recognition or sensitivity whatsoever of anyone they might be studying regarding the "interior silence" which Cartier-Bresson knew was always present in undertaking a photographic portrait.

H. G. Gadamer has indicated that science "gives the appearance of being total in its knowledge," but it refuses "to exclude all that which actually eludes its own methodology and procedures . . . in this way [it] provides a defense behind which social prejudices and interests lie hidden and thus protected" (1977, 93). This is Carlyle's nescience. What we learn from the traditional statistical portraits of leaders is devoid of the compassion that propelled someone like Gandhi to heroic action, social justice activism, and nonviolent revolution. Without an understanding and recognition of human interiority and its dynamics with beliefs, values, and in Gandhi's case religion, I doubt we will ever be able to prepare the kind of leaders some critics advocate to undertake "deep change" or "deep democracy" in schools. To do that we will have to recognize the limitations of science and to take current criticisms of the "lack of rigor" in conducting research about educational leadership as often excessively narrow and even sterile (Levin 2006). When some critics who argue for conducting more "robust research" in our field admit that their antidotes are not very radical and don't "shift our thinking without being too uncomfortable to live with" (see Seashore Louis 2007,

240), I am skeptical about what "robust research" might really portend and why we would consider it desirable.

I am reminded of the comment by Niels Bohr, the Danish physicist and winner of the Nobel Prize, on the value of really good theories. Bohr insisted that good theories had to be "really crazy" and violate "common sense in a fundamental way" to have any chance of making an important discovery (Gratzer 2002, 42). One indicator of the value of more "robust research" might be that the theories that shape it strike us as "really crazy" and cause a great deal of discomfort. I suspect, though, that the definition of "robust research" has to do more with statistical reliability and efficiency than the breakthrough dimension sought by Bohr.

In reviewing what constitutes the impact of artistic works in the world, S. Schama echoed Bohr's sentiments:

> The power of art is the power of unsettling surprise. Even when it seems imitative, art doesn't so much duplicate the familiarity of the seen world as replace it with a reality all of its own. Its mission, beyond the delivery of beauty is the disruption of the banal. Its operational procedure involves the retinal processing of information, but then throws a switch and generates an alternative kind of vision: a dramatized kind of seeing. (2006, 7)

In addition, Jurgen Habermas's criticism of some of the work done by Talcott Parsons seems apropos here, that there was a large imbalance between his categorical containers and "the slight empirical content housed in them" (1991, 188). Much of the content produced by narrowly defined empirical studies, though perhaps "rigorous" in the sense they adhere to the rules of classical empiricism, yield precious little content about the nature of leadership in schools or otherwise.

And I am not at all sure there is not a touch of dogmatism involved with some admonitions about "robust research," for as Gadamer noted about Martin Heidegger's thought: "That science originates from an understanding of being that compels it unilaterally to lay claim to every place and to leave no place unpossessed outside of itself. But that means that today not metaphysics but science is dogmatically abused" (1983, 163).

THE LIMITATIONS OF A PURELY SCIENTIFIC APPROACH TO THE STUDY OF LEADERSHIP

Under the current theoretical limitations we have imposed upon our preparation programs in educational leadership, we would, most likely not find much in the way of Gandhian compassion to be an explicit mission. Those urging us to expand "research rigor" would I think, in the main be unconvinced that such a line of inquiry would lead to anything that could be tangibly linked to the quest for improved student "outcomes." That is testimony to the extent we have been transformed and transfixed by the business rhetoric of efficiency that dominates our working milieu and which has moved us away from an ethic of service and constructing civic capacity and what P.Houston has called "the spirit of commonweal" (2006, 5) to a market-centered view of schooling dominated by the profit motive (see Crow, Hausman, and Scribner 2002, 204–7).

And while the push to link principal behaviors to student outcomes is replete within the ISLLC/ELCC (Interstate School Leaders Consortium/Educational Leadership Constituent Council) standards, there is no recognition that administrators do not work directly with students, that the research regarding leadership effectiveness must include teachers as the intervening variable, and that by doing so the authoritarian, one-way, top-down model of leadership is reinforced and legitimated in such an assertion. Alternative models of leadership that proffer more egalitarian viewpoints are thus delegitimated by the standards.

M. Bottery has written extensively about the forces of standardization and control at work in education leadership today. He downplays the perspective of Marx in deconstructing socio-political-economic issues and proffers Max Weber's emphasis on the increased ubiquity of rationalized and bureaucratic processes and structures, with their stress on efficiency, calculability, predictability and control . . . when the ultimate aim is that of making a profit, then the more efficient the structures, the more likely profits will be generated . . . and such efficiency . . . is greatly facilitated by . . . high degrees of specialization, hierarchical authority structures with restricted command and responsibility, an impersonality of relationships, the recruitment of individuals on the basis of ability and technical knowledge, and the application of impersonal rules to all that explains the actual manner of production. (2004, 78)

When Weberian rationality is coupled with Taylorian methods of job deskilling, the profit motive is enhanced. Within this perspective empiricism works effectively. The major issue facing preparation programs becomes one of fitting graduates into more highly rationalized work structures. It is what Houston meant when he said of school system leaders today, "The business community wants superintendents to be more like them" (2006, 5).

Bottery's (2004) view has been reinforced by observations from Larry Cuban: "What business-inspired reformers wanted for state and local curricula, tests, and 'bottom line' accountability has largely been achieved at the cost of preserving orthodox school organization and conventional teaching practices that an earlier generation of business-led reformers severely criticized as both traditional and regimented" (2004, 111).

We have lost sight of Dewey's distinction between leadership as knowledge and leadership as art in the limited empiricism or opinion cloaked in the formulation of the ISLLC/ELCC preparation standards, that despite their verbiage to the contrary have nothing to do with performance and the art of practice. Performance, in all of its subtlety, is concerned with application, art if you will, and it is usually embedded in a variety of moral or value discourses. These are Dewey's "non-rational factors" cast out by scientific discourse as nonmeasurable or unimportant (by their exclusion from consideration), but which firmly anchor value orientations such as compassion that swim in larger moral discourses. The current ISLLC/ELCC standards substitute open-ended "evidences" as descriptors of "the level of performance" without ever describing the actual perform-ance itself. Thus, the "art" of leadership has no face, force, or hu-manity in such criteria (see Hessel and Holloway 2002 for how per-formance is enunciated). It is a view of leadership once described by Chris Argyris as one in which "the variable human seems to be min-imally variable and minimally human" (1972, 33).

Using figure 1 as a reference for this discussion we are left with only the cognitive side of leadership embedded in scientific empiri-cism where the major problem is not performance but definition (see Rost 1991). It would be similar to describing the impact on an audi-ence of an opera singer such as Leontyne Price by saying she received a forty-two-minute standing ovation (the evidence) as Leonora in *Il Trovatore* (1999) without ever describing *what* she did to receive such

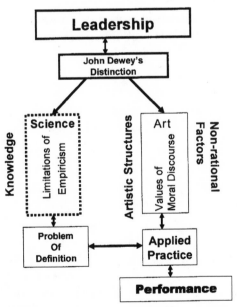

Figure 1. *Dimensions of Leadership*

a tribute. And how would a leadership program deal with Price's self-description embedded in her own moral discourse?

> I think we performers are monsters. We are a totally different, far out race of people. . . . My proudest moment . . . was my debut at the Metropolitan. It was my first real victory, my first unqualified acceptance as an American, as a human being, as a black, as an artist, the whole thing. . . . Art is the only thing you cannot punch a button for. You must do it the old-fashioned way. Stay up and burn the midnight oil. There are no compromises. Accomplishments have no color. (1999, 48)

I argue in leadership preparation that informing a student that he/she might receive a standing ovation for performing such and such a task leaves the actual performance of the task masked and unpacked. I proffer in my most recent book (English 2008) that practice is about performance, and practice is not likely to be improved with more of the same kind of science (more precise definition) we have historically employed. Improved application begins by placing it within Dewey's "artistic structures" concept where the integrity, subtlety, and the true forceful impact of leadership reside.

This is the missing ingredient in most educational leadership preparation programs with which I am familiar, and it is largely absent in the existing standards we use to prepare leaders. I think that the most telling criticism of the standards is not that they are centered on practice but that they have little to do with practice except in the crudest sense. And they have little if anything to do with establishing an educational leader's personal sense of identity, place, and context, which is vital to lead an organization effectively. I can't imagine any preparation program giving someone the insight and courage to say, as Leontyne Price remarked:

> Once you are on stage, everything is right. I feel the most beautiful, complete, fulfilled. I think that's why, in the case of noncompromising career women, parts of our personal lives don't work out. One person can't give you the feeling that thousands of people give you. I

have never given all of myself, even vocally, to anyone. I was taught to sing on your interest, not your capital. (1999, 48)

Figure 1 helps me pose this question more clearly. If we acknowledge that the practice of leadership, its performance, envisioned either as public portraiture rendered in a shifting and fluid decision dynamic (what some researchers refer to as "complex" scenarios, see Levin 2006) and/or a theatrical rendition or public presentation (see Starratt 1993; Furman and Starratt 2002), then we can only understand it and prepare educational leaders to work within it by reconsidering "artistic structures" as the essence of applied practice. And our research strategies must similarly be altered to flesh it out. Rather than rigor being defined by exclusion of the art of leadership embedded in a variety of moral discourses, "robust research" must be envisioned as inclusionary. Then if our brand of "science" will not enable us to understand this more encompassing perspective of leadership as an art form, we must face up to the fact that our science prohibits us from coming to a more complete understanding of what we want to know. If we cannot permit ourselves to fully comprehend the nature of leadership because of how we have chosen to define or view it, we should stop using methods and models that leave us perpetually ignorant and unable to adequately grasp what expert practitioners who are supremely artful performers really do.

P. Johnson described the dilemma in this manner:

Leadership is an empirical phenomenon conducive to study from a descriptive social scientific, and value-free standpoint. As such, it is aptly approachable through the methods of sociology, psychology, and political science (among others). It is also an inherently humanistic concern whose ambiguities, contextuality, and normativity require the interpretive methods and devices of history, literature, and philosophy (among others). No account of leadership can be complete, or completely adequate, unless it makes some explicit attempt to integrate these two methodological perspectives. (1996, 13–14)

Perhaps Gandhi said it best when he wrote,"I claim that human mind or human society is not divided into watertight compartments called social, political and religious. All act and react upon each other" (Attenborough 1982, 75).

I will return to the science/art dichotomy again. Before doing this, I want to acknowledge the insights of T. B. Greenfield (Greenfield and Ribbins 1993) when he pointed out that the arts are not subservient to the sciences but represent "unique insights in their own right" (256). He went on: "For me the arts are not . . . to serve the propositions of social science. . . . Much more the arts speak to questions of how to live life. People who make policy based on what social science tells them will need something more. They would do well to call on the humane vision that the arts can give" (257).

PART 3

One View of the Historical Moment in Educational Leadership

Next, what I should like to do is provide a perspective of what I believe to be the "historical moment" in educational leadership. Aspects of this analysis have appeared in many publications over the past six years (English 2001; 2002; 2003a; 2004; 2005; 2006b; 2007), but this is the first time in which I have collected all of them along with some different pieces of that moment for presentation and discussion.

Figure 2 reveals what I am choosing to call "The Nature of Ideologies in Scientific and Professional Discourse."

Originally the term "ideology" was created by Destutt de Tracy for the analyses of ideas emanating from sensory inputs (Boas 1984, 156). Karl Marx appropriated the idea to refer to the "false consciousness" of a specific social class (Sterba 1999, 416).

Today "ideology" is used by laypersons and scientists alike as a term to connote something that has the trappings of science but is actually pseudo-science (Boudin 1989). However, science and ideology are not two separate processes, for as Boudin explains, the creation of ideologies is a natural part of the scientific process (1989, 91). J. Watt (1994) indicates that "any statement about the world must be framed in terms of one repertoire of conceptual schemes or another" (185), and therefore, "any scientific question or conclusion must exist within the framework of one ideology or another" (87). But it isn't only the question of conceptual frames, it is also a question of the hidden influences of the adopted frame or frames. The reason is as Lewontin explains:

> The problems that science deals with, the ideas that it uses in investigating those problems, even the so-called scientific results that come

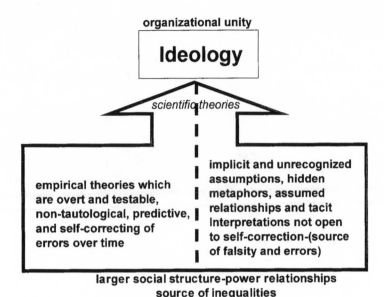

Figure 2. *The Nature of Ideologies in Scientific/Professional Discourse*

out of scientific investigations, are all deeply influenced by predispo-
sitions that derive from the society in which we live. Scientists do not
begin life as scientists . . . but as social beings immersed in a family,
a state, a productive structure, and they view nature through a lens
that has been molded by their social experience. (1991, 3)

Lewontin (1991) also warns us that one of the social purposes of
science is that of explaining how things work not only to scientists
but to the general population. When science tends to support the existing social institutions, especially in a society where wealth and
power are distributed unevenly, then "that is . . . when we speak of
science as ideology" (4). The purpose of explaining the existing relationships maintained by social institutions amounts to *legitimation*,
"irrespective of the practical truth of scientific claims" (5).

What appears as scientific may in fact be an ideology. The influ-
ence on scientists is pervasive and subtle: "It comes in the form of
basic assumptions of which scientists themselves are usually not

aware yet which have a profound effect on the forms of explanation and which, in turn, serve to reinforce the social attitudes that gave rise to those assumptions in the first place" (Lewontin 1991, 10).

I have repeatedly pointed out that in descriptions of the preparation standards for educational leaders we have avoided raising these issues (English 2000; 2003a; 2003b; 2004; 2005; 2006b). I want to do so once again as a matter of illustrating some of the ideologies at work in the creation of the standards, the assumptions made about the existing role of schools in our society, and the assumptions rendered about the theories in use and the concept of a knowledge base, which is central to the creation and political sustenance of the standards.

I proffer that the creation of the standards and their utilization in accreditation, a policing function, represents an exercise in politics and power first, and second, to a much lesser extent, an exercise in empiricism and professionalism. I also want to argue that the standards are laced with ideologies regarding efficiency as the paragon of leadership practice as exemplified in the world of commerce and profit and point us away from what J. R. Wiens has called "civic humanism" (2006, 223) and E. A. Samier (2007a) identifies as a "public service ethos." As such, leadership in schools embodied in these standards will reinforce existing social and economic inequalities in the larger social fabric. In short, they lead us away from social justice. While they may embrace *caring*, they are devoid of *compassion* in the Gandhian sense.

However, in this examination I want to underscore that consideration of the interolocking agencies and agendas comprising an ideology is, as J. Watt indicates, "neither true nor false itself, but it [an ideology] can accommodate a domain of true statements about the world (as well as a domain of false statements)" (1994, 185). My point with the examination is not whether the statements comprising standards are true or false but that if we are going to use them *as if they were true*, we understand the epistemological, conceptual, and practical problems if they prove not to be, and that we consider the distinct possibility that many may not be, true.

I see little willingness at the moment to even consider the possibility and the implications. Such questions are overwhelmed by the requisite political requirements to engage in accreditation, licensure, and a variety of other for-profit activities in the marketplace, such as holding copyrights and profiting from the fees derived from licensure testing. To admit that some of the content of the preparation standards may not be true is politically untenable and undermines a host of other activities and assumptions.

The notion of an interlocking ideology represented in figure 2 comes from B. Dunham's *Heroes and Heretics: A Social History of Dissent* (1964). Dunham indicates that organizations have their own special "ideology." It consists of a special need to explain and support their activities and actions: "They must do this for their own members, who, otherwise, might doubt the value of membership. They must do it for non-members, with a view to recruiting or to being tolerated" (15).

Dunham proffers that organizational ideology consists of three types of claims. The first are assertions that "describe the objective circumstances in which the organization acts and stating the moral values which the organization regards as ultimate" (15). The second assertions regard the purpose of the organization and its structure. The third claims involve how the purposes of the organization are to be achieved within its circumstances. What these three sets of claims do is establish a foundational platform for action. Dunham states:

> It is plain that an organization which, in its ideology, lacked any of these three groups of sentences would be unable to explain or justify its existence and actions. Without a description of objective circumstances nothing can be explained; without a demonstrable system of values, nothing can be justified. Without a statement of purposes, it cannot be known what the organization intends; without a program, it cannot be known how the purposes are to be attained. (1964, 16–17)

The ultimate function of an ideology is to create unity within the organization. The binding of members together within an organization is therefore intimately related to cohesive shared intentions, or as Dunham declares, "So long as this intent exists, unity will follow. What organizations fear is loss of the intent" (1964, 17).

I see in Dunham's presentation the rationale that supports program standards in educational administration as stipulated by J. Cibulka (2004). The Cibulka statement is all about the need for unity, the need to agree on standards to promote quality with the accompanying accreditation mechanism with analogies to law and medicine. Cibulka says, "I contend that the debate [regarding standards] should not be about *whether* to have standards but *how to write those standards* and *how to enforce them*" (2004, 4). So Cibulka is not so interested in the actual content of the standards as in the need for them so that enforcement is possible. In figure 3 this is represented by the concept of a stable political platform on which rest licensure apparatuses, accreditation agencies, copyright holders, testing companies, and a variety of pro-profit activities where organizations make money from the standards.

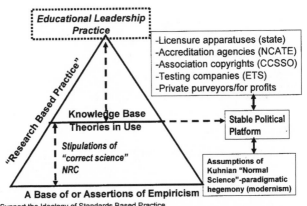

Requisite Assertions to Support the Ideology of Standards Based Practice
1-theory bashing-minimize or eliminate multi-paradigmatic inquiry as unnecessary-downgrade role of the university
2-create a "leadership crisis"-attack "harmful monopolies" and "the faulty pipeline"-recast social change as
    social turmoil and threats to political stability and control by current political elites
3-use business ideologies/metaphors to recast the dilemma as one of inefficiencies and not public service
4-use standardized tests as a method to support the claim schools and current leadership are "failing"

Figure 3.   *The Interlocking Ideology of Standards-Based Practice and Its Principal Beneficiaries*

Cibulka's (2004) rationale is about the loss of intent and the loss of unity because without a stable political platform these are in jeopardy. But the rub comes in the actual formulation of the standards, for as Dunham describes:

> Human beings have all sorts of limitations, and are therefore prone to error. Their senses, which connect them with the environing world, are not inclusive enough nor penetrating enough, even when helped with scientific apparatus, to present the world accurately in any single moment or series of moments. Men are therefore thrown back upon ratiocination to amend the incurable defects of the senses . . . alas, the intellect is brief in attention, prone to illogic, and subvertible to prejudice. Thus we sometimes assert what we do not know, and we sometimes do not know what we assert. (1964, 17)

The result, according to Dunham, is that organizational ideologies may contain very deep errors. However, once they are embedded in an ideology they become extremely difficult to correct because "their removal is not a mere scientific adjustment but a dislocation of the corporate body" (1964, 18). It is my contention that this is where we are with what has been accomplished with standards-based practice in this historical moment. I want to take the occasion, using figure 3 as a reference, to indicate where potential sources of error can be located in the interlocking ideology that binds all of the work accomplished together. In this respect Alan Wood's remark about the work of Bertrand Russell is prescient when he said, "The way to clarify controversial questions is by 'a more careful scrutiny of the premises that are apt to be employed unconsciously, and a more prolonged attention to fundamentals'" (1995, 197).

THE IDEOLOGY OF EMPIRICISM

At the stem of the interlocking ideology shown in figure 3 are claims about empiricism. In his analysis of post-Galilean empiricism, P. Feyerabend (1995) indicates that science is *critical* in that it allows revision to occur based on new data. This means that it possesses the capacity to become self-correcting, though new views may have to overcome initial resistance. At the same time, however, Feyerabend points out that "this critical practice is accompanied by a *dogmatic ideology*" (1995, 34). The dogmatic aspect of empiricism is that "it is assumed . . . All theories rest on one and the same stable foundation, *experience*. It is experience which supports, and gives content to, our ideas without itself being in need of support and interpretation" (34).

These presuppositions form the base of empiricism. Can there be a foundational base for empiricism that is itself not empirical? And even more importantly, Can such a foundational base remove doubt and establish certainty on which an empirical theory rests? H. G. Gadamer recalls that "the justification of knowledge, in the sense of a certitude removed from all doubt, was an impossible task" (1983, 163). At stake in this critical nexus is the relationship between assertions regarding what is truth and the nature of truth as derived from experiences. If there is no foundational level to empiricism other than faith, on what basis can experience be judged to be true or not if the answer is not within empiricism itself?

Charles Sanders Peirce (1955) dealt with the issue of using faith or revelation as a source of knowledge and certainty. Faith pretends to offer certainty, but Peirce noted three objections. Paraphrased, they were, first, that humans can never be absolutely certain that any given assertion is truly warranted. Second, such assertions can never be supported by reasoning. Finally, the foundation of faith cannot really be established as ultimately true. For these reasons Peirce noted that faith (or revelation as he called it) "far from affording us any certainty, gives results less certain than other sources of information" (1955, 57). If the foundation of empiricism is faith, the certainty we often ascribe to it, even if our research procedures are accurate, should be similarly circumscribed to a little less certainty, at least.

Karl Popper has argued that there is no way that scientific theories can be confirmed, justified, or verified empirically. However, he has proffered that they can be falsified, but not necessary empirically. Rather they are falsified by basic statements that may be influenced by empirical means but are not necessarily empirical themselves (1968, 43).

When only human experience is proffered as the means by which one can determine if something is true or not, several problems arise. S. Haack indicates that "we cannot always perceive clearly, that we sometimes misperceive, that our senses can be fooled . . . we may, if inattentive or flustered, fail to see what is before us, that we may not recognize, or may mis-identify what we see, hear" (1996, 110).

Haack also acknowledges that there can be "pervasive interpenetration of background beliefs into our beliefs about what we see, hear, etc." (1996, 110). In short, there is no "context-free" method of "seeing" anything.

My point in opening this very brief exploration is not to discredit experience or even empiricism as a method of knowing. The point is to show that the possibility of error is very large in empiricism generally and in science specifically. Also, there is an ideology present in scientific activities consisting of the presuppositions and assumptions upon which experience is identified, culled, and categorized and that observation is usually theory-embedded and not theory-free.

> The idea that information concerning the external world travels undisturbed via the senses into the mind leads to the standard that all knowledge must be checked by observation: theories that agree with observation are preferable to theories that do not. This simple standard is in need of replacement the moment we discover that sensory information is distorted in many ways. We make the discovery when developing theories that conflict with observation and finding that they excel in many other respects. (Feyerabend 1993, 234)

The relevance of this brief exposition is to show that to make claims that practices should be incorporated into a knowledge base which is then molded into a stable political platform for accreditation, licensure, and other for-profit activities because they represent "research-based practice" is likely to contain large errors and flat-out dead ends, even if the "rules" of "correct science" have been followed (English 2007). J. Murphy has admitted in the construction of the ISLLC standards that "no one associated with the ISLLC has ever claimed that the Standards are 'actually true'" (2000, 412). This admission is telling because it means that not only were the framers of the standards working within a variety of ideologies which were not questioned as either scientific nor nonscientific but that they were either unaware or unconcerned about codifying bad practice in the process, even when it represented the "wisdom of the field" (412).

As I will try to point out in the next section, it does matter if we know how truthful our claims are in codifying professional practice. It does matter if we have some idea of how our presuppositions have shaped our perceptions prior to observation. It does matter if our recommended knowledges, skills, and values pertaining to leadership preparation reinforce or challenge the existing socio-economic-political strata in which schools currently are located and reproduce. And if we don't really know what is true within these activities sketched out in figure 3, how should our doubts be expressed? How much certitude is acceptable and in what ways in the preparation of educational leaders? What this revelation means is that wrapped within the empiricism embodied in the ISLLC/ELCC standards are any number of ideologies. Here is G. Canguilhem's reminder of the problem:

> For many scholars the notion of scientific ideology is still controversial. By it I mean a discourse that parallels the development of a science and that, under the pressure of pragmatic needs, makes statements that go beyond what has actually been proved by research. In relation to science it is both presumptuous and misplaced. Presumptuous because it believes that the end has been reached when research in fact stands at the beginning. Misplaced because when the

achievements of science actually do come, they are not in the areas where the ideology thought they would be, nor are they achieved in the manner predicted by the ideology (1988, 57–58)

I would like to illustrate this dilemma with an example from the medical profession. an applied field to which we are frequently compared (see Cibulka 2004). I call it "the Pasteur problem."

PART 4

The Pasteur Problem

The ISLLC/ELCC (Interstate School Leaders Consortium/Educational Leadership Constituent Council) standards represent a distillation of what is believed to be good practice(s) in educational leadership. The standards have been posed as representing "the core technology" of school leadership (Murphy et al. 2000). So what the standards represent are codified beliefs, actions, and procedures that the framers believed defined good practice (see also Hessel and Holloway 2002; Shipman, Queen, and Peel 2007). These standards are partially derived from empirical research and partially from "the wisdom of the field" (Murphy 2000). In addition, the proposed standards were subjected to an examination linked to a validation of the content of the *School Leaders Licensure Assessment* (the *SLLA*) (Tannenbaum 1997). The content had also been derived from a national job analysis study of the beginning school principalship (Tannenbaum 1996) and later the superintendency (Lantham and Holloway 1999).

The "Pasteur problem" is one that links the discovery of a solution to medical practice to a nonmedical problem. Louis Pasteur, a chemist, was involved in a study of certain mineral substances via crystallography. He was employed by the French wine industry to determine why some wine went bad. In his work on tartaric and racemic acids, Pasteur separated chemical compounds in the process of fermentation caused by living microorganisms (Porter 1999, 431-35). Pasteur became the first to link "germ, fermentation, and disease in a unified theoretical framework" (Canguilhem 1988, 70). The impact on medical practice was profound:

> Thus crystallography revealed to Pasteur the structural novelty of the living organism: its asymmetry. Medical practice, which at the end of

the century would finally begin to deliver on promises that medicine had made through the ages, acquired new efficacy as a result of research whose fundamental concern could not have been more remote from those of the medical practitioner. (Canguilhem 1988, 70)

The "Pasteur problem" is simply this. No amount of codification of medical practice or even research within practice would have produced anything remotely approaching modern medicine prior to Pasteur. His research had nothing to do with medical practice. He was not even a medical doctor. If one could have taken a survey of the very best medical practitioners within the two hundred years prior to Pasteur, one would not have anything close to modern medicine or medical practice today by distilling their "wisdom of the field." Surveys of practice by practitioners may contain significant ideologies that go unquestioned and are passed off as the epitome of professionalism. It is possible then to enshrine bad practice in the process of attempting to upgrade it.

It seems to me that the methods used in verifying practice for the ISLLC/ELCC standards offer us no assurance that the practices we believe are good are, in fact, *true*. We have no assurances that a different set of practices might not be better, and we have no real grasp of the extent to which ideologies are mixed in with our perspectives and our "science" as they have been in most other scientific fields over time. We forget that mathematics was at one time as concerned with symbols and the mysteries of numbers, along with astrology, as in what we consider the domain of mathematics today (see Aczel 1996). Psychology contained theories of the soul and the life of the spirit. Chemists were also concerned about applications of alchemy (Canguilhem 1988, 28).

The apparatus we have constructed to create standards for educational leadership as illustrated in figure 3 offers us no guarantee that standards-based practice will lead to the kinds of results that medical practitioners promised their patients hundreds of years prior to Pasteur but couldn't deliver.

Empirical data are theoretically useless without a theoretical specification of the conditions under which the data are valid and how they ought to be used. In order for science to make use of data collected in the course of preexisting practice, that practice must be translated into conceptual terms; theory must guide practice, not the other way around. The gap between theory and practice is often wide. Yet no theory ever emerges from empirical practice alone. (Canguilhem 1988, 110)

My line of argument is that in order for us to practice accreditation, create and politically support licensure apparatuses, protect copyrights, and enable some agencies to make a profit by opening the preparation of educational leaders to the marketplace, it was and remains necessary to create a stable political platform. To admit that the apparatus itself is unwieldy, contains ideologies at every juncture, and even contains falsity amounts to heresy. None of the agencies involved with licensure, certification, and testing of potential candidates for leadership positions wants anything to do with admitting that the ISLLC/ELCC standards are not stable and enduring, because their authoritative positions in the anatomy of professional preparation require such permanency.

And the fact that practitioners have offered no criticism of the standards cannot be evidence that they contain no errors (Murphy 2005, 168). Ideologies are often invisible to practitioners: A long list of examples abound in the medical literature regarding medical practice in which doctors found no reason to change their practices even when empirical evidence strongly suggested they were not only detrimental to their patients but often resulted in their deaths (see Duffy 1979; Nuland 2003; Haggard 2004).

Medical practitioners particularly have worked to reinforce the social biases and prejudices of the larger society in their practices across many centuries and indeed continue into modern times as revelations of medical interns strongly indicate continued social prejudices against women and persons with different sexual orientations and even persons who are obese (see Klass 1987; Erdmann 2005; Holman 2005).

In his 1999 the American Educational Research Association (AERA) invited address on educational leadership, J. Murphy describes in some detail the context he sees as the "ideological footings of the emerging sociopolitical infrastructure" in which "the one piece of the foundation that shines most brightly is . . . 'the ascendancy of the theory of the social market'" (1999, 9). Indeed, the ISLLC/ELCC standards reflect such "ideological footings" deeply intertwined with the compatible ideology of total quality management (Anderson 2001). The ISLLC standards are thoroughly penetrated with market ideologies favored by neoconservative critics of current educational leadership preparation programs (Broad Foundation 2003; Hess 2003; Emery and Ohanian 2004; Weiner 2005).

Arguments centered on the necessity for standards to engage in aspects of professionalism and connections to quality practice (Cibulka 2004) are secondary for me, because they fail to deal with the issue that undergirds the entire apparatus itself. How do we know, without an obvious Pasteur present, that our codifications of "good practice" are in fact "good"? What evidence is there to support the notion that professional preparation is not doing what medical doctors did for a thousand years after the encyclopedic works of Galen (c.130–c.200): simplify, copy, and pass on erroneous concepts and practices that inhibited medical progress until the sixteenth century? (Porter 1999, 73–82).

Galen proffered that the preparation of a physician began with the mastery of philosophy and that "anatomical phenomena" reflected "the teleology of a divinely ordered universe" (Porter 1999, 75). While Galen wrote sixteen books on the human pulse, his anatomical musings were based on animal dissections that erroneously attributed to humans the same organ properties as those found in pigs or apes. He fully justified bloodletting as an antidote to a vast array of human ailments. And as Porter noted, "his teachings on plethora [a body condition believed to be characterized by excess of blood marked by turgescence and a florid complexion] and venesection [the opening of veins for the purpose of bleeding] remained influential until the nineteenth century" (1999, 77). It is clear from historical appraisals of medical practice over the ages (Nuland 1988; Gordon 1993; Porter 1999) that it has been thoroughly permeated with ideologies at every level and in each epoch of practice (Ball 2006), and remains so to this day, even after Pasteur (see Porter 2003; Takakuwa, Rubashkin, and Herzig 2005).

Educational leadership also suffers from the thorough penetration of sociopolitical ideologies of the "power players," and they are reflected in our standards of preparation, licensure, and accreditation. Much of the work of scholars in educational leadership in the past five to seven years within the University Council for Educational Administration (UCEA) has been to expose and change such ideologies under the rubric of social justice (Rorrer 2002; Alston 2005; Shoho, Merchant, and Lugg 2005; K. M. Brown 2006; Crow 2006). Far from being a separate agenda from performing purely "empirical research," a binary that has been put to me on more than one occasion, the confrontation and exposure of the ideologies that are embedded in our assumptions are part and parcel of how research is defined and the uses to which it is put. T. Monahan (2005) has phrased it succinctly. Instead of asking Does it work? we should be asking What social relations does it produce? (8). That to me is the central issue in an anatomy of any professional practice.

PART 5

Contested Notions of "Correct Science"

Recently there has been an effort to codify and sanctify scientific investigation and to separate practices, some of which, in the opinions of some, are better than others (see National Research Council 2002). The temptation to elevate some forms of inquiry over others has a long history in the West, but attempts to rationalize and make logical what is illogical have led to few actual scientific breakthroughs. Over a half-century ago, Cambridge scientist W. I. B. Beveridge commented about the limitations of reason and logic in scientific work: "Our conception of science has been given us by teachers and authors who have presented science in logical arrangement and that is seldom the way in which knowledge is actually acquired" (1950, 109).

Nobel Prize–winning chemist Max Perutz similarly said, "Scientists rarely follow any of the scientific methods that philosophers have prescribed for them" (1995, 56). Paul Feyerabend and Imre Lakatos (Motterlini 1999) both rejected empiricism and the way science was supposed to work by performing historical case studies of how actual scientific discoveries were made. They found that actual scientific breakthroughs did not follow the scientific method or exact procedures as specified by philosophers for those discoveries.

J. LeFanu examined the "ten definitive moments" in medicine, ranging from the discovery of penicillin in 1941 to the helicobacter in 1984. First, LeFanu notes that "scientists alone could never have invented or created them [antibiotics] from first principles" (14). The discovery of penicillin was not a result of science or rationalism, the kind advocated in the codifications of "correct science" (LeFanu 1999, 15). In fact LeFanu indicates that medicine's postwar success was "built on chance discovery" and not on the systematic pursuit of rational processes within known theory bases (340). LeFanu indicates that all of the chemicals used to fight cancer today "owe their origins to chance observation or luck" (112). And LeFanu calls "clinical science" an ideology and notes that the welfare of the patient became subordinated to the "progress of science" (171). Statistical clinical trials utilizing large quantitative data in epidemiological studies "are likely to be pseudo-explanations":

> It is this statistically derived knowledge that has consistently been shown to be unreliable, promoting the patently absurd as proven fact. Further, clinical trials cannot answer the sort of complex questions that frequently crop up in medical practice and when many are aggregated together, incomplete data is run through computer programs of bewildering complexity to produce results of implausible precision. . . . This form of knowledge . . . has been shown to result in the adoption of an ineffective treatment in 32 percent of cases and the rejection of a useful treatment in 33 percent of cases. (LeFanu 1999, 362–63)

The self-encapsulated process of "research-based practice" shown in figure 3 and in more detail in figure 4 indicates why more "rigorous research" is not likely to lead to any startling breakthroughs in practice except refinements of what is already known. That was certainly the case in medicine and largely remains so today. The decried lack of "rigor" of research in educational leadership and the paucity of the results we do obtain from it (see Levin 2006; Honig and Seashore Louis 2007) are not merely a criticism of the purity or fidelity to what is commonly believed to be good research practice but of remaining thoroughly inside the extant empirical/theoretical base. As in medicine, the theoretical base of Galen led to no new medical breakthroughs until it was supplanted. That is why contemporary "theory bashing" is so antidiscovery and prosociopolitical status quo. When J. Murphy (1999; 2002) declares that "the belief that better theories will be the savior of educational

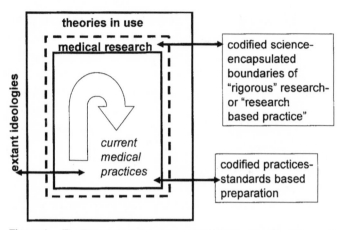

Figure 4.   *The Encapsulated Anatomy of Teleological Practice/Research and Research Based Practice*

practice. . . is a little like the case for cold fusion" (1999, 48), the result is the reification of practice as we know it, the enshrinement of the ideologies which support it as the pinnacle of that practice, and the creation of an antichange doctrine in the guise of preparing practitioners. It ignores the actual history of breakthroughs in medical practice where life-saving medical discoveries were never the result of freezing the theoretical status quo harder for new knowledge (LeFanu 1999). No new knowledge milked from the existing theoretical base produced the breakthroughs in the first place (LeFanu 1999, 340). They were, to use T. S. Kuhn's terminology, nearly always out of "paradigm" (1996, 10).

But such a stance does ensure the political stability of what has been defined as the "knowledge base" to support the remainder of the agencies and institutions that require certitude and permanency to exercise their authority in professional circles.

As in the case of medical research, "rigorous research" normally means improving statistical probability within what is perceived to be empiricism. Such a science is applied within the extant and accepted "theories in use" and are mutually reinforcing in medicine and in educational leadership. The ends and the means are one and the same. Science is defined by its methods, and methods in turn define science. Only empirical theories "work" in this approach, and standards represent codified "research-based" practices verified empirically. It has been my position that such an approach is not likely to yield any new discoveries regarding educational leadership (English 2007). The history of medical breakthroughs demonstrates the limitations to discovery. What figure 4 does show is that social science has constructed what in art would be called "formalism," where no matter what the actual object looked like, it would be rendered in about the same way (see Feyerabend 1996, 149). I believe that we have reached a certain kind of "formalism" in conducting behavioral studies of leadership. Continued application of the same assumptions and methods will not enable researchers to come any closer to what we want to know about leadership (see Stein and Spillane 2005). It is my contention that until and unless we use Dewey's concept of "artistic structures," our inquiry is not likely to yield many new significant discoveries.

PART 6

An Anatomy of Professional Practice

From the previous discussion regarding current issues with standards-based practice and the apparatus that has been put into place to promote it, figure 5 abstracts the key components in an attempt to depict the discrete but interlocking elements of the "anatomy of professional practice." The importance of understanding such an "anatomy" is to link the elements advanced by proponents and critics into a subsequent model that shows how changes in one element impact upon others. It is also an attempt to show which elements are foundational and which represent the superstructure of leadership practice.

Proponents of the ISLLC/ELCC (Interstate School Leaders Licensure Consortium/Educational Leadership Constituent Council) standards rarely delve into the epistemological claims and the attendant theories in use upon which their assertions regarding the knowledge base or the standards derived from that base are inextricably derived (Shipman, Queen, and Peel 2007). This hiatus is revealing. By not acknowledging the problematic nature of the epistemological assumptions, which by necessity have to be erected to support any standards, proponents never have to confess to the temporality of their claims, never have to deal with the thorny issues of how such standards have been determined to be truthful beyond a measure of popularity, and never have to confront the ideologies in which the standards swim. This means that the issue of social justice is muted in the schools and the profession because it is only with the acknowledgment of the ideological sculpting of the standards that social justice issues become relevant. Eschewing such conversations as unnecessary and/or unproductive (Murphy 1999;

39

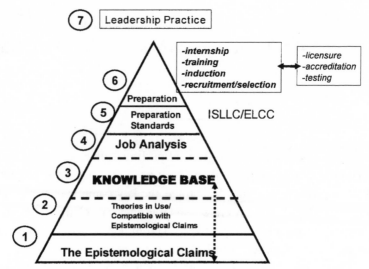

Figure 5.   *An Anatomy of Professional Practice*

2002), the line of argument moves to the anticipated "benefits" of possessing a knowledge base and the attendant autonomy associated with practicing professionals, often using medicine and law as examples (Cibulka 2004).

Figure 6 indicates that ideologies are present at virtually every component/level in the anatomy of professional practice. Although some researchers and critics of research in educational leadership scold us for not separating values from research-derived fact (see Levin 2006), no less than Richard Lewontin, a leading geneticist at Harvard who holds a prestigious chair in zoology, makes it abundantly clear that it is impossible to separate the dominant social and economic forces from shaping what scientists do and how they think. Science is thus a form of ideology, a system of belief that is value-based and "comes in the form of basic assumptions of which scientists themselves are usually not aware yet which have profound effect on the forms of explanation and which, in turn, serve to reinforce the social attitudes that gave rise to those assumptions in the first place" (Lewontin 1991, 10).

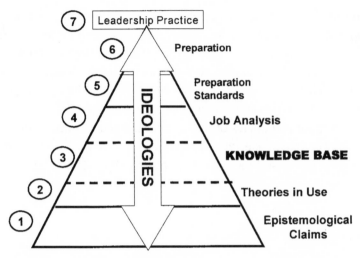

Figure 6.   *The Presence of Ideologies at Each Level of Professional Practice*

Leadership is an embedded act within the existing currents of socioeconomic beliefs and practices in capitalist America. It has been pervasively racist (Tillman 2003; F. Brown 2005; Dantley 2005; Murtadha and Watts 2005), sexist (Ortiz and Marshall 1988; Blount 1998; Shakeshaft 1999; Mahitivanichcha and Rorrer 2006), and homophobic (Sears 1993; Capper 1999; Lugg 2003; Lugg and Koschoreck 2003; Blount 2005) since its inception and remains so. It has been highly influenced by American business practices almost since its origination in university graduate programs (Callahan 1962; House 1998; Saltman 2000; Cuban 2004), and the notion that somehow research about educational leadership could become sterilized against such attitudes is impossible (see Tillman 2002; Young and Lopez 2005). If it is, according to Richard Lewontin (1991), impossible for biology, which is not an applied discipline, how then would it be possible for educational leadership, which is an applied field?

The continuing struggle in our own field against these pervasive ideologies remains a huge obstacle to creating a more effective public-school administrative cadre (Wiens 2006). The density of the beliefs and the metaphorical structures connected to them have a long history in Western metaphysics and continue to serve as the cornerstone of white racism, which is encapsulated in "the creative fusion of scientific investigation, Cartesian philosophy, Greek ocular metaphors and classical aesthetic and cultural ideas . . . as true representations of reality" (West 1999, 75). C. Schmolders (2000) also vividly demonstrates how Nazi aesthetic ideological physiognomy supported policies of racist exclusion and extermination. And the sciences have especially been guilty of promoting racism in their categorizational schemes in natural history (West 1999, 77).

PART 7

Exploring Cognitive Aesthetics
and the Zone of Transference

In probing the potentialities for more fertile perspectives in studying educational leadership and in extending John Dewey's concept of "artistic structures" (1964/1926, 144), figure 7 presents a somewhat different view on the relationship sketched out in figure 1. Figure 1 indicates that Dewey's distinction between science and art may be viewed as a clean separation. I will argue that in fact there is a kind of "zone of transference" in which the clean distinctions are very much blurred. I will argue that it is within this "zone of transference" that some of the most promising arenas exist for the study of educational leadership in the future (English 2008).

By "transference" is meant a junction between science and various artistic structures where science takes on the form and substance of art, and where artistic forms begin to look, feel, and resonate more and more like science. Lawrence-Lightfoot and Hoffman Davis (1997) spend time discussing this intersection, presenting vignettes of those scholars whose work could be classified as "boundary crossers," such as William James, John Dewey, and W. E. B. DuBois (6–7). They proffer that DuBois's work particularly "organically integrated science, art, history and activism" (7).

P. Atkinson (1990) indicates that to cleanly separate science and art because the former represents measures of "facts and exactitudes" while the latter stands for "aesthetic" and "subjectivity" would amount to letting oneself "be hoodwinked by uncritical everyday prejudices" (10). Such a separation represents a "gross over-simplification" (10). Both science and art "are predicated upon the texts of everyday life" (10). Both perspectives draw upon

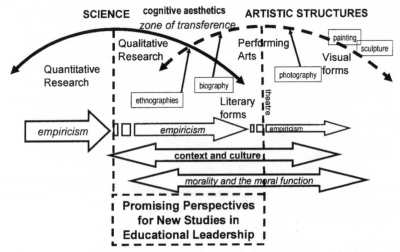

Figure 7.   *Cognitive Aesthetics and the Science/Art Transference in a Study of Educational Leadership*

"a stock of cultural codes and conventions" (11), and J. Clifford (1986) observes that "the making of ethnography is artisanal, tied to the worldly work of writing" (6).

H. F. Wolcott (1999; 1995) speaks of ethnographic fieldwork as a kind of artwork in which he indicates there is the *ethnographer-as-artist* and the *ethnographer-as-craftsperson.* The former role is aligned with actual fieldwork and its interpretation, which are artistic, while the latter is centered on writing about fieldwork (Goodall 2000, 169). Ethnographers, as social scientists, use observation, interviews, and personal experiences, as wel as commonly referenced abstractions, recognizable forms or genres, and professional standards for regulating relations (Goodall 2000, 169).

It would be difficult to dispel Wolcott's notions of ethnography from a classic painting done by Vincent Van Gogh entitled *The Potato Eaters,* completed in 1884–1885 (Schama 2006, 312). Van Gogh desired to create art not only which was truthful, but which represented the context and cultural conditions of his subjects. The colors Van Gogh selected were "the unrelieved hue of mud, muck, and soil, the material from which these people are themselves constituted" (Schama 2006, 311–12). M. Kieran also notes that *The Potato Eaters* "sought to evoke an imaginative understanding of the harsh living and working conditions the peasants were subject to" (2005, 103). Van Gogh achieved this reality "through a particular labouring and abstraction of style that brings home the rough, coarse, brutal aspects of their lives" (103). The same result of ethnography may be obtained as desired by Van Gogh: "We are being encouraged, via artistic means, to conceive of the peasantry as morally beautiful and good in virtue of their harsh conditions and relations to the soil" (104).

R. H. Brown has written about "the rhetoric or poetics of sociology" (Atkinson 1990, 19). Brown employs the idea of *cognitive aesthetics* to reconcile art and science and to appreciate "the aesthetic dimension of sociological knowledge" (1977, 3). Brown would unite science and artistic structures shown in figure 7 into a unitary framework. Part of his rationale is that all of the social sciences "are permeated with metaphorical usages" (102) and that the "failure to recognize the metaphorical character of 'scientific' language leads one to mistake the proper metaphorical nature of theories, models and representations" (102). Brown also argues that even quantitative research employing "analytic induction, controlled comparison, hypothesis testing, and inference can thus be seen as unselfconscious names for what may be understood as aspects of metaphoric thinking" (125).

Figure 7 shows that the ideology of empiricism is still at work in cognitive aesthetics because, as Kieran indicates, for humans, "experience is a primary means of understanding. We come to discriminate, appreciate and grasp many things on the basis of experience" (2005, 191–92).

We must have experienced, in some sense, the bad in order to understand the good. Someone whose life is utterly charmed, who has never experienced betrayal, deceit, tragedy or failure, may be able to appreciate many things, but it is unlikely they will really know certain things about friendship, love, morality or great art. (Kieran 2005, 192)

These experiences contain commonly understood cultural symbols and signs, mythologies, and other cultural narratives that inform both the processes and products of inquiry in science and art.

Dewey believed that the moral function of art "can be intelligently discussed only in the context of culture" (1958/1934, 344). Dewey then indicated that "the sum total of the effect of all reflective treatises on morals is insignificant . . . becoming important [only] when 'intellectual' products formulate the tendencies of these arts and provide them with an intellectual base" (345). These products are "attended by the flourishing of the arts that determine culture" (345). Dewey declared that "art is more moral than moralities" (348) and that it was "imaginative experience" that "constitutes the heart of the moral potency of art" (349). Then he laid out that platform which extends a study of educational leadership beyond the kind of behavioral quantification that has been the hallmark of so many "leadership studies" of surveys and checklists: "Art is a mode of prediction not found in charts and statistics, and it insinuates possibilities of human relations not to be found in rule and precept, admonition and administration" (349).

SOME BENCHMARK EXAMPLES OF COGNITIVE AESTHETICS IN EDUCATIONAL LEADERSHIP RESEARCH

Figure 8 represents an enlargement of the zone of transference shown in figure 7. Inserted in figure 8 are benchmark examples of types of educational research and writing that would be representative of a range of cognitive aesthetics. Many of these will be familiar resources to readers.

It is my contention here and elsewhere (see English 2007) that this type of research/scholarship is most likely to lead to discoveries in educational leadership. It isn't that the traditional quantitative methods are not valuable, but given their limited ability to include the full

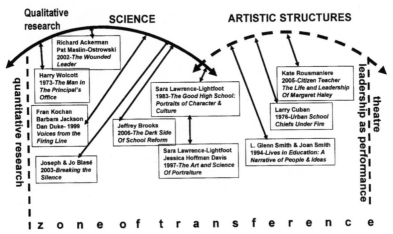

Figure 8. *Some Benchmark Examples of Cognitive Aesthetics in Educational Leadership Research*

range of human emotional and value orientation variation, context sensitivity, and inclusion of the moral function, it is unlikely that their continued application will be the repository of any new breakthrough understandings in educational leadership. Because human leadership is a culturally enveloped, contextually specific interaction, studies that eliminate such variables because of the research lens employed are not likely to include the "Pasteur moment." It is much more likely that such moments will come from a more inclusive range of studies represented in the idea of cognitive aesthetics, because paradigm expansion and juxtaposition are more likely here than in the narrower epistemology and methodology of quantitative or even some mixed method studies. After discovery, however, quantitative research may prove invaluable and necessary to verify the breakthrough. In short, quantitative methodologies are appropriate for studies that aim to verify existing practices or outcomes; they are not likely to produce new practices or spark original insights outside of them.

To satisfy my own curiosity on this matter beyond the limited books that dot our field, some of which are shown in figure 8, I turned to a review of manuscripts submitted and then published in the University Council for Educational Administration's (UCEA's) premier journal, *Educational Administration Quarterly*. First, I was interested in knowing about the actual current intellectual thought in the field and what might be considered to fall into the category of cognitive aesthetics. I defined a published piece that might be considered cognitive aesthetics as containing one or more of the following components derived from R. H. Brown (1977, 61–62):

- makes use of a variety of individual points of view, perhaps borrowing a specific individual's "angle of vision" when it suits the purposes of the piece or the nature of the inquiry;
- utilizes a dramaturgical or theatrical technique of "showing not telling" and momentarily becoming "objective" within this perspective;
- engages in generalizations from narratives using critical comments;
- assumes a panoramic view of events, presenting a narrative of "simultaneous happenings or sometimes disassociated scenes that a narrator-agent could cover only by the use of the most improbable devices" (61);
- discovers, describes "multiple traits and facets of characters (or cultures) under study readily and plausibly without having to work things around to bring any single point of view within discovery range" (62).

These criteria present a kind of counterintuitive positioning of research in our field that would most likely suffer rejection under all kinds of guises but is most strikingly not the kind advocated by the National Research Council (2002) as "rigorous" in education (English and Furman 2007).

From data submitted to the UCEA Executive Committee by D. Pounder and R. Johnson (2007) the number and percent of manuscripts submitted in 2005–2006 by type are shown in table 1:

Table 1.   Manuscripts Submitted in 2005–2006 to *Educational Administration Quarterly* by Type

Type	# New	% New	# Revised	% Revised
Quantitative Empirical	49	36.8	14	43.75
Qualitative Empirical	58	43.6	14	43.75
Mixed Empirical	3	2.3	2	6.25
Conceptual, nonempirical, "from the field"	20	17.3	2	6.25
Total	133	100	32	100

Note: Data extrapolated from D. Pounder and R. Johnson's memo to the UCEA Executive Committee, February 13, 2007, p. 2.

Table 2 shows the number and types of articles accepted for publication in *Educational Administration Quarterly* for 2004–2005 and 2005–2006.

For the next step in this process I reviewed all fifteen issues of *Educational Administration Quarterly* for 2004 through 2006 and classified them by major methodological perspective. These are shown in table 3.

The data in table 3 indicate that the dominant methodological perspective represented in the published articles in *Educational Administration Quarterly* for 2004–2006 was quantitative analytical processes followed by pieces which were primarily reflective or conceptual, literature reviews, or polemical in nature. The third

Table 2.   Manuscripts Accepted for Publication in the *Educational Administration Quarterly*, 2004–2006, by Type

	2004–2005		2005–2006	
Type	#	%	#	%
Quantitative Empirical	1	12.5	3	30
Qualitative Empirical	6	75	4	40
Mixed Empirical	0	0	1	10
Conceptual, nonempirical, "from the field"	1	12.5	2	20
Total	8	100	10	100

Note: Data extrapolated from D. Pounder and R. Johnson's memo to the UCEA Executive Committee, February 13, 2007, p. 2.

Table 3.   Major Methodological Classification of Published Articles in
Educational Administration Quarterly, **2004–2006**

Year	Issue	Total	Quantitative	Qualitative	Mixed	Other*
2004	August	5	4	1	0	0
2004	October	6	0	1	0	5
2004	December	5	3	2	0	0
2004	February	6	1	0	0	5
2004	April	8	0	0	0	8
2005	August	6	3	3	0	0
2005	October	7	0	3	0	4
2005	December	3	1	2	0	0
2005	February	5	2	2	0	1
2005	April	5	2	2	1	0
2006	August	6	4	1	0	1
2006	October	5	1	3	0	1
2006	December	5	3	0	1	1
2006	February	5	0	5	0	0
2006	April	3	3	0	0	0
	TOTALS	80	27	25	2	26
			(34%)	(31%)	(2.5%)	(32.5%)

Note: *conceptual, reflective, review of the literature, polemical articles

major category was represented by qualitative methods. However, the three categories were summatively very close.

To determine if any of the published pieces in *Educational Administration Quarterly* could be classified as examples of cognitive aesthetics using R. H. Brown's five criteria, each of the eighty published pieces in *EAQ* was reviewed to determine if they included one or more of the criteria and, if so, which major methodological perspective(s) was employed in them. The purpose of the review was to determine which methodological approach would most likely include aspects of cognitive aesthetics.

These data are shown in Table 4.

Of the fifty-five published pieces examined in fifteen issues of *Educational Administration Quarterly* (2004–2006) and which included one or more of Brown's (1977) criteria for sociological content being labeled an example of cognitive aesthetics, qualitative approaches were clearly able to include more of the criteria. In fact, since the largest number of published articles in *Educational Ad-*

Table 4.   Published Articles* in _Educational Administrative Quarterly_, 2004–2006, that Included One or More of the Criteria for Cognitive Aesthetics, by Major Methodological Perspective

Method	Criterion 1	Criterion 2	Criterion 3	Criterion 4	Criterion 5	
	"Angle of Vision"	"Showing Not Telling"	"Narrative Generalization"	"Panoramic View of Events"	"Multiple Traits and Facets"	Totals
Quantitative	3	0	6	0	1	10
Qualitative	20	10	21	9	18	78
Mixed	1	1	2	0	1	5
Other	13	1	16	4	7	41
TOTALS	37	12	45	13	27	134

Note: Of the eighty published articles, fifty-five (69 percent) contained one or more of Brown's criteria for cognitive aesthetics.

ministration Quarterly were primarily quantitative in nature (see table 3), the contrast between the two approaches is striking overall. None of the published quantitative pieces dealt with the utilization of a dramaturgical or theatrical technique of "showing not telling" and momentarily becoming "objective" within this perspective (Brown's criterion 2, 1977), or assuming a panoramic view of events, presenting a narrative of "simultaneous happenings or sometimes disassociated scenes that a narrator-agent could cover only by the use of the most improbable devices" (Brown's criterion 5).

The purpose of this discussion is not to show the "superiority" of any method of inquiry over any other method in conducting research in educational leadership. It is, however, to show that methods have embedded limitations in what they allow to be considered legitimate topics for research. Quantitative research, at least as represented in the published articles in _Educational Administration Quarterly_ for the time period examined, was more likely to define the topics more narrowly, adopted stricter views regarding theoretical borders, was less open to adopting varying angles of vision, confined "objectivity" solely within the stipulated framework employed, was less apt to seriously question generalizations or conclusions derived from the data reported, was more likely to present data serially as opposed to simultaneously, and at the conclusion of the reported research activity, usually moved to squeeze the data gathered into a single point of view congruent with the theoretical or conceptual lens employed at the outset of the research activity.

When verification of existing variables and dimensions are not to be seriously questioned but the purpose is to test them or ascertain their relationships within known settings and ranges of variance, this approach makes sense. It is straightforward and economical. However, when discovery is the purpose of the inquiry, when the conceptual borders are less certain or even to be questioned, when actions, actors, and activities are viewed as more complex and fluid, and when the research activity is to consider the moral and value implications of events, decisions, and interactions, then a wider angle of vision that reflects less certitude is in order, for as C. S. Peirce observed, "Oftentimes it is precisely the least expected truth which is turned up under the ploughshare of research" (1955, 55). And when the purpose of the research activity is to understand the widest range of complexity at work in various settings in which humans must work, interact, and, in the case of educational leaders, render decisions and simultaneously consider their moral values, the research activity moves away from symbolic certitude to methods that encourage a wider panoply of possibilities and potentialities. It is then that we can observe the movement toward the arena of cognitive aesthetics. Of the eighty articles reviewed in *Educational Administration Quarterly* in the time period 2004–2006, 69 percent utilized one or more of R. H. Brown's (1977) criteria for cognitive aesthetics, but only ten (12.5 percent) met at least four of those criteria. These articles are listed in the appendix.

It seems reasonable to believe that if educational leadership as a field currently contains someone like a Pasteur at work, she or he is more likely to be working in the zone of transference than anywhere else. This area is arguably the most open to unexplained phenomena and the most open to even seeing them in the first place. One does not usually observe what one does not expect to find. And in the case of educational leadership, a most complex and nuanced activity within a peculiar social/moral enterprise, this perspective seems entirely reasonable, for as sociologist Michael Mann has observed, "No laws are possible in sociology . . . for the number of cases is far smaller than the number of variables affecting the outcome" (2003, 341). Approaches which are open to the most inclusive lens on variation within leaders as they function in culturally specific contexts are more likely to contain chance discovery such as those that have been noted in the advance of medical practice (see LeFanu 1999).

PART 8

Leadership as Drama, Theater, and Performance

Some forms of inquiry in the social sciences push into the arena of theater, even using dramaturgical metaphors. For example, it is common for social science researchers to refer to their subjects as "actors" (see also Lawrence-Lightfoot and Hoffman Davis 1997). A recent award-winning article by M. Song and C. G. Miskel (2005) spoke of influential policy actors within social network theory. They quote K. S. Cook, who indicated, "No single theoretical perspective will enable us to explain everything about organizational interaction" (1977, 77), and B. G. Peters, who remarked, "Some eclecticism of approach is likely to pay greater intellectual dividends . . . than is a strict adherence of a single approach" (1999, 2). Rusch (2005) studied institutional barriers to organizational learning and employed the concept of "system scripts." Within the concept of "new institutional theory" E. A. Rusch discerned four types of district-level scripts in which district administrators maintained a code of silence regarding innovative schools in school districts.

R. J. Starratt discusses the intersection between science and art in terms of the concept of structuration theory advanced by A. Giddens (1984). Structuration theory posits that a "sociology of action" evidences a duality in which "action is shaped by structure but at the same time action produces or reproduces structure" (26). In this dynamic nexus where human leadership is situated, "structure is both the medium and the product of action" (Starratt 1993, 26).

Starratt posits that in organizational life, members are searching for ontological security because they are faced with imposed constraints and the need or requirement to exercise creativity and accomplish tasks within or despite such constraints (1993, 28). The role of leadership is to negotiate the spaces between the constraints, securing compliance from others as to the necessary changes to enhance organizational productivity within the appearances of continuity (35). This dynamic represents a form of drama or theater, for as Starratt notes, "In a multiplicity of circumstances and social systems, individuals are reading cues and codes, interpreting symbolic expressions at several levels, and improvising responses every day" (41).

A key border-crossing work in our field is *The Wounded Leader* by Richard Ackerman and Pat Maslin-Ostrowski (2002). It builds on the requirement of the leader to "negotiate space," as in Starratt's analysis, except that in the lens created by Ackerman and Maslin-Ostrowski, when the constant need to work in contested space results in contradiction to the psychic needs of the leader, a "wound" results in which there are real emotional cuts that may lead to actual physical distress. The disjunction between who the leader is and what the leader perceives himself or herself doing to lead creates a personal crisis.

One such crisis in the life of a national educational leader was recounted by Terrel Bell. Bell was U.S. Secretary of Education in the Reagan administration (1981–1984). He found himself having to defend budget cuts to his own department. These cuts were going to take away aid to college students, the disadvantaged, and the poor. Bell recounted:

> I was going to have to defend these indefensible cuts. . . . I dreaded the scenes when it came time for appropriation hearings in the House and the Senate. My colleagues in education knew that I knew better. I could read the scorn on their faces. Here was a contemptible little white-haired man acceding to the betrayal of the nation's schools and colleges. (1988, 68–69)

Bell recounts packing his belongings once again in a U-Haul truck and heading home with "a nagging feeling of betrayal . . . promises

I thought had been made had not been kept . . . frustration at not having been able to secure an enduring commitment to the cause of education at the highest federal level" (162). Clearly, Ted Bell displayed all of the signs of a wounded leader. And the source of our knowledge about it came from an autobiography, one of the oldest literary forms in the human experience.

What can be seen in figure 7 and figure 8 within the zone of transference is that certain forms of qualitative research in the social sciences "cross over" into a space where both in content and in form they begin to resemble art. For example, in the articles reviewed in the *Educational Administration Quarterly* that contained at least four criteria cited by R. H. Brown (1977) relating to cognitive aesthetics, we see the researcher as a third party using quotations from subjects who were speaking in the first person (see appendix a). The reader becomes a third party examining the data. Table 5 shows the similarity between scientific form that crosses over into "cognitive aesthetics" and the theater as a representative example of an artistic structure.

What is also confounded within the zone of transference is the mixture of traditional notions of objectivity and subjectivity in forms of social science research and what has been considered forms of literary and performing arts (see English 2006a).

S. J. Maxcy (1994) has described the growing awareness of Americans that leadership contains an embedded aesthetic component. He calls this an "oversight" inherited "from Kantian philosophers who separated knowledge from values. As a result, modernist administrators dealt with art, often reluctantly, only as non-rational" (1994, 157).

Table 5. Zone of Transference/Cognitive Aesthetics

Observational Perspective	Social Science Research Form/Qualitative	Artistic Structure/Theater
Observer	Researcher (3rd person)	Playwright (3rd person)
Observed (data)	Actors (1st person)	Actors (1st person)
Intended recipient(s)	Reader (3rd person)	Audience (3rd person)

What we see in some emerging educational leadership as published in *Educational Administration Quarterly*, at least within the last three years, is a continuing movement into what has previously been considered artistic forms, because it is within these realms we can explore issues of moral leadership and values as they exist in educational institutions and agencies at all levels. This extension of our research is key to social justice and democratic community, for as G. Furman and R. Starratt remind us:

> Since democratic community is *moral*, leadership practices proceed from this moral sense. It is intentional leadership aimed at enacting the values of democratic community; sociality for its own sake; open inquiry in pursuit of the common good; a deep respect for individuals; celebrating difference; and a sense of interdependence with all life. (2002, 124)

It is these issues of leadership as an embedded moral enterprise located and intimately connected to one's sense of personal and historical identity within a specific culture that can be studied. Perhaps the purest form of a narrative line, which is sometimes a moral commentary within an artistic structure, is hip-hop music, which "joins features of black oral culture, especially toasts (long narrative poems) and the dozens, to a variety of black musical styles" (Dyson 2004, 425). It is also true, but not necessarily as clear, that nearly all forms of research are also connected to the researcher's personal and historical identity within a specific culture and assume a line of narrative (see Tillman 2002).

In a recent book entitled *The Art of Educational Leadership* (English 2008), I described leadership as a performing art. There may be a science of leadership, but in its application, leadership is performance. The same would hold true of medicine or nearly every other applied professional field. Especially "doing leadership" is artful performance since there is no science of application. One of the problems of the kinds of standards for leaders we have today is that they are primarily definitions of what constitutes the tasks of management, but they do not deal with the act of leading in an educational institution. In short, our leadership standards are not about leadership at all. They are, rather, about managing functions, tasks, and responsibilities in schools as they currently exist. Artful performance is nowhere to be found in them.

While artful performance is the key to effective leadership, it is also the key to being a competent trial lawyer. There is certainly a knowledge component in practicing law. The content of laws and judicial decisions are exceptionally important when constructing a case or crafting a brief. But the practice of cross-examination is an art form. It marks the difference between what Francis Wellman has called a good office lawyer and a competent trial lawyer. A good cross-examiner "should be a good actor" because, as he cautions, "The most cautious cross-examiner will often elicit a damaging answer. Now is the time for the greatest self-control. If you show your face how the answer hurt, you may lose your case by that one point alone" (1962, 33). Wellman, who was considered one of the greatest trial lawyers of his time, sketched out what it took to practice the art of cross-examination:

> a habit of logical thought; clearness of perception in general; infinite patience and self-control; power to read men's minds intuitively, to judge of their characters by their faces, to appreciate their motives; ability to act with force and precision . . . an extreme caution; and, above all, the instinct to discover the weak point in the witness under examination. (28)

The ability to perfect this art involved "all shades and complexions of human morals, human passions, and human intelligence" (Wellman 1962, 28). No such language like this appears in our standards for educational leaders. And because educational leadership is about morality and values, the moral imagination has to become a centerpiece of leadership development and practice, though Maxcy renames this aspect of artful performance as "democratic value deliberations" (1991, 111–30).

My own observation is that most preparation programs today are centered in the functionalism and managerial efficiency mental prisms embodied in the total quality management (TQM) ideology reinforced by ISLLC (Interstate School Leaders Licensure Consortium) and ELCC (Educational Leadership Constituent Council) standards (see Shipman, Queen, and Peel 2007) and NCATE (National Council for Accreditation of Teacher Education) accreditation than in matters of developing moral imagination. Maxcy's concept of "artist-leader" has yet to be seriously considered as a model for leadership preparation, despite his rationale that "administration in general, and educational administration in particular, is art—because life is art, or should be practiced as art" (1991, 193).

T. B. Greenfield and P. Ribbins stake out a similar perspective in envisioning academic preparation from an artistic standpoint: "The most valuable form of training begins in a setting of practice, where one has to balance values against constraints—in which one has to take action within a political context . . . only somebody who has acted this way is ready for true training in leadership" (1993, 257).

The implications of considering leadership as artful performance instead of as a factotum carrying out functional managerial tasks is profound. The ultimate aim, according to Greenfield and Ribbons, is not to make philosopher-leaders, but to make leaders "philosophers, or artists maybe" (1993, 257). The end result would be "to make them more humane in any case, more thoughtful of their power, more aware of the values it serves or denies" (257). Preparation in the arts, and I would add research about leaders from artistic perspectives, "could also give leaders an insight into motive and intention and the operation of will and the relationship between each and all of these things and actions" (260).

T. E. Deal and K. D. Peterson (1994) talked about the role of the principal as one involving the wearing of bifocals. They indicated that leadership involved balancing logic and artistry in schools and living with paradox. Some became "artist principals" who sought to "define reality, capture and articulate symbols that communicate deeply held values and beliefs, and engage people in ritual, ceremony, theater, and play" (1994, 8). Their purpose in doing so was to create layers of meaning "that makes school a place of the heart, as well as of head and hands" (8).

D. L. Duke analyzed the aesthetics of leadership in which he showed that "acts of leading" could be considered works of art, and very much as in the case of artistic endeavors, unless a perceiver/receiver was involved in the act(s) it went unrecognized because an "observer must find something about a leader meaningful" (1989, 352). Duke divided leadership aesthetics into the categories of *dramatics, design,* and *orchestration.* Similarly, these categories contained the properties of *direction, engagement, fit,* and *originality* (352).

On the dimension of originality Duke admits that "leadership by nature . . . defies generalizability and predictability . . . [because] no 'one best' style of leadership exists . . . each set of circumstances is unique—with a different configuration of actors, and a meaning all of its own" (1989, 357). In the realm of ritual and ceremony, leadership represents dramatic performance. As performance, leadership includes such things as *image, voice, setting,* and *timing* (358). And echoing an earlier theme I raised, Duke notes that if leadership is concerned with meaning and values, "then prospective leaders may derive great benefit from a classical liberal arts education" (362).

While my review of published articles in the *Educational Administration Quarterly* for the time period 2004–2006 revealed that a majority possessed some of the attributes of cognitive aesthetics, some of these are not completely absent in some forms of quantitative research, and I was not able to find an unmistakable trend line toward broader aspects of studying the complexities of educational leadership qua cognitive aesthetics. It is my hope that this text will encourage such a trend, because I firmly believe that there are not likely to be any new true discoveries about leadership without such an expansion.

PART 9

Aesthetics, Morals, and Evil in Leadership

One of the dilemmas in studying and understanding leadership is what Barbara Kellerman has called the problem of "Hitler's ghost" (2004, 11). This is the conundrum of ignoring bad leadership because it doesn't fit scientific studies or we don't want to admit that bad and good leadership emanate from the same sources and involve the use of the same skill sets. Kellerman looks at Hitler and asks, "His use of coercion notwithstanding, if this is not leadership, what is?" (11).

P. Johnson speaks to this "dark side" of leadership and comments:

> It simply won't do, as some scholars have attempted, to define leadership in such a way as to preclude its being used to denote the practices of those whose effect upon the people who fall under their influence is harmful or otherwise untoward. We need, rather, to bring all forms of leadership under scrutiny and to incorporate into our analysis of its various methods and manifestations a specifically moral-theoretic component. (1996, 13)

One sees rather clearly that only an aesthetic approach to understanding a leader such as Hitler remotely comes close to grappling with the issue of evil. Evil is not a scientific question. It is a moral question, and there is no science of morality. Social science research can examine leadership as effective or ineffective, positive or negative, transactional or transformational, innovative or traditional, open or closed, humanistic or mechanistic, but aesthetic judgments include questions of morality where the issue of evil can be broached. I am struck by the tragedy of the lack of morality in the testimony of Albert Speer, Nazi secretary of armament, who, when asked about his view of Nazi forced laborers, remarked that he loved machines more than people. Speer said that human suffering "influenced only my emotions, but not my conduct" (1970, 70), and he confessed that what bothered him more than his conviction at Nuremberg was that "I did not see any moral ground outside of the system where I should have taken my stand" (70).

The presence of evil in a leader such as Hitler raises profound issues in coming to grips with the impact of leadership. R. Rosenbaum likens Hitler's evil to an art form because it embodied "a knowing awareness of wrongdoing" (1998, 215). And Hitler presented himself to the German people as "a mythmaking artist rather than as a politician" (217). The Nazi program has been characterized as "a demonic art that tried to sculpt a racist idea of perfection from the flesh of the genome through primitive biogenetic engineering that entailed euthanasia, eugenics, and mass murder as racial sculpting tools" (218). Inquiries such as Rosenbaum's (1998) are examples of aesthetic scholarship. Such queries are simply outside the rules of science. Yet without this added dimension, how can the full scope of leadership ever be grasped? E. Heller indicates that Nietzsche found art superior to science in grasping truth because, "for him, the conceptualization of knowledge and truth is essentially an aesthetic function—even scientific knowledge's source lies in intuition" (Samier and Stanley 2006, 41).

One of the few books in educational administration that tackles bad leadership which in some aspects borders on evil is Joseph Blasé and Blasé's exploration of how school principals mistreat teachers by belittling them or withholding or denying them opportunities, resources, or credit. Such actions may includes spying on them and sabotaging their work, and it may escalate to unwarranted reprimands, unfair evaluations, and forcing them out of their jobs (2003, 140). Another example is Jeff Brooks's *The Dark Side of School Reform* (2006).

Eugenie Samier is also exploring something she calls "the shadow side of compassion" by studying the covert practices of secrecy and tradecraft in educational administration. Her scholarship is extremely creative as she is creating a theory based on the Jungian concept of "the shadow as a metaphor for the covert organization." The tradition she is bucking in her line of inquiry is that schools

> tend to exclude those practices involving clandestine activity such as intelligence gathering, surveillance, sabotage, misrepresentation, resistance and disinformation against both members of the organization and other organizations. It is the covert side of the organization that is arguably the most difficult challenge for leadership in both overcoming its practices and negative effects and avoiding these practices themselves in a highly politicized and changing environment. (2007b, 2)

What the aesthetic dimension brings to a picture of leadership is a much fuller understanding of the nature of truth in representation and presentation. I refer here to Jacque Derrida's work *The Truth in Painting* for an explanation that I also believe applies to research in educational leadership. Derrida indicates that there are four dimensions that comprise "the truth in painting." The first pertains to the "truth in painting," which means that the truth *in the painting* is "the truth of the truth" presented without a mask. The second pertains to the idea that the "truth" is faithfully represented so that it is in fact the "double" of itself. The third idea of the truth is that as an art form, the truth is faithful to that form. Derrida calls this "the art of the signatory" (1987, 6). The final interpretation is that the truth is represented as true within the art which is called pictorial.

We can draw parallels with conducting research regarding educational leadership. The first is the "truth" in research, that is, the truth of the truth in research. The second is whether the truth has been faithfully presented in the research method selected. The third is the truthfulness of the researcher in conducting the research. The final meaning is the truth as it regards research, that which is true and which is reported as research.

If the truth about educational leadership is only partially represented, then it can't be the truth of the truth. If research fails on this criterion, all the other forms of truth representation are also compromised, though what is investigated may be faithfully presented and the researcher himself/herself may be truthful to a specific form of research. The fact that the truth of the truth is only half-represented distorts any subsequent presentation of it. I believe that Derrida's distinctions represent an index as to why, if we fail to include all that we understand leadership to be in our researching of it, we do a disservice to artful leaders who are masters of their craft in fully comprehending what they do, and we shortchange our students who are depending on us to prepare them for the full panoply of challenges they will confront in the schools.

PART 10

Summing Up

These are the major points that I believe are important in summing up the line of argument proffered in *An Anatomy of Professional Practice*:

1. PROFESSIONAL STANDARDS MUST REVEAL THEIR EPISTEMOLOGICAL CLAIMS REGARDING TRUTHFULNESS TO BE JUDGED USEFUL TO THE FUTURE OF A PROFESSION.

For professional standards governing preparation and accreditation practices to be considered useful in the long run in the life of a profession, they must reveal their claims to truthfulness, that is, their epistemology must be delineated. Professional consensus is not enough and cannot be a substitute to establish truthfulness. The cumulative experiences of practitioners cannot be an arbiter on this dimension, for as Charles Sanders Peirce put it, "Direct experience is neither certain nor uncertain, because it affirms nothing—it just is" (1955, 57).

The "wisdom of the field," which has augured large in the creation of current educational leadership standards (Nicholaides and Gaynor 1989; Murphy and Hawley 2003; Murphy 2005), has assumed the kind of certitude and universality that belies its fragility and temporality. Rational procedures alone cannot be a substitute for truthfulness. Once again, Peirce noted, "There are three things to which we can never hope to attain by reasoning, namely absolute certainty, absolute exactitude, absolute universality. We cannot be absolutely certain that our conclusions are even approximately true" (1955, 56).

John Dewey remarked that the major factors determining the empirical form of education were "tradition, imitative reproduction, response to various external pressures wherein the strongest force wins out, and the gifts, native, and acquired, of individual teachers" (1929, 14–15). In this latter category Dewey indicated that there was a "strong tendency" to equate teaching ability with methods that brought "immediately successful results," defined as "correct recitations . . . passing of examinations and promotion of pupils to a higher grade." This image of professionalism was dominant in the minds of the community and of the students who wanted to become teachers. Dewey remarked that such graduate students wanted to "find out how to do things with the maximum prospect of success. Put baldly, they want recipes" (15).

To a far greater extent the standards in use today for the preparation and accreditation of educational leaders rest on recipes as well. We have no idea if they are true (Murphy 2000) and no idea if they even represent effective leadership. A codification of practices is, as Peirce put it, simply a codification that affirms nothing.

Knowing if the underlying epistemology of practice represents truth or not is the key to dealing with the problem of hidden ideologies present in them. The current leadership standards are replete with such ideologies including large doses of the ideology of total quality management (TQM) (English 2004; 2008).

2. SOCIAL JUSTICE ISSUES ARE NOT TANGENTIAL TO THE PRACTICE OF EDUCATIONAL LEADERSHIP, BUT PART AND PARCEL OF RIDDING PROFESSIONAL STANDARDS AND PRACTICES OF DETRIMENTAL IDEOLOGIES AND NEGATIVE STEREOTYPES.

I continue to hear criticism from educators, some professors, and practitioners that concerns about social justice are not part of the "main agenda" of educational leadership preparation. The false binary is presented as, "When are we going to deal with the real issues of leadership which are student achievement or making schools more effective?" *instead of* matters of racism, sexism, homophobia, and the like. I would remind these critics that educational leadership has been embedded with deep and historic prejudices against African Americans, Latinos, Asians, women, and homosexuals.

These evils are well documented in our literature. Rooting out these historic and deleterious prejudices against marginalized groups amounts to an assault on the ideologies that permeate every field and are not unique to educational administration (see Takakuwa, Rubashkin, and Herzig 2005 for the battle against them in medical education) but which are especially damaging and hurtful to a profession entrusted with the protection and care of children.

Social justice issues are not only intertwined in our profession and within professional preparation programs but they are ensconced in our schools where educational leaders have responsibilities to create a safe environment free from bullying, oppression, and marginalization of all children. We cannot continue to pollinate prejudice in our preparation programs or stand by and watch their propagation in the schools. The conspicuous silence that surrounds them in the ISLLC/ELCC (Interstate School Leaders Licensure Consortium/Educational Leadership Constituent Council) standards (Shipman, Queen, and Peel 2007) is an abrogation of the first order in creating more democratic schools and a just society.

The ISLLC/ELCC standards represent a discourse, and they are presented as a "given" not open to question (Shipman, Queen, and Peel 2007). Their existence is taken as a sign that they are truthful as presented. As Usher and Edwards (1996) note, a discourse that functions like this "operates behind their backs, it is an unthought. It is not itself questioned although it is the means by which questions are asked. One consequence of this is that discourses not only constitute objects but 'in the practice of doing so conceal their own invention'" (Foucault 1974, 49).

3. THE CONCEPT OF A KNOWLEDGE BASE SHOULD BE REPLACED BY THE IDEA OF A KNOWLEDGE DYNAMIC.

A knowledge base in a field of professional studies rests on assumptions regarding stability, internal consistency, and uncontested borders in which a "field" is separated from a "nonfield." There is no empirical method for determining these borders, because a line of demarcation between science and nonscience, a field and a nonfield, a "core" and a "noncore" is ahistorical and unsustainable except in the rawest of public arenas where such issues can be papered over with political power (Lakatos 1999; English 2002; 2004). A "knowledge dynamic" acknowledges that defining the borders between an applied field and a "nonfield" is not the central issue, because the growth of knowledge is not about privilege and power, exclusivity and elitism, but about truthfulness and problem solving, and rests on theoretical pluralism and creating competing research programs (Lakatos 1999). This position stands in stark contrast to elevating only one form of inquiry as legitimate in fostering and sustaining research monopoly (National Research Council 2002).

4. RESEARCH ABOUT EDUCATIONAL LEADERSHIP IS NOT LIKELY TO LEAD TO MANY NEW SIGNIFICANT DISCOVERIES UNLESS IT INCLUDES AESTHETICS AND THE TRADITIONS OF THE HUMANITIES (THE MORAL DIMENSIONS).

Leadership studies, especially in educational administration, have largely ignored central moral issues in schooling because they are sanitized or erased in the method of inquiry that has come to dominate the field. There are two dimensions at least in advancing the case for aesthetics and aesthetic inquiry in our research into leadership. The first stems from the notion that organizational life not only produces cultural artifacts such as stories, rituals, and ceremonies (Smircich 1983), but that organizational work is essentially about using symbols and language in aesthetic constructions. Leadership itself represents a distinguishable form of an aesthetic construction (Samier, Bates, and Stanley 2006). In the words of Ernst Cassirer, "Art gives us order in the apprehension of visible, tangible, and audible appearances. . . . The infinite potentialities of which we had but a dim and obscure presentiment are brought to light" (1956, 213).

The second is that bad leadership involves moral dimensions that are best analyzed within aesthetic traditions. Science sanitizes such leadership dimensions. But aesthetics can encompass a full range of mismanagement and evil in leadership. While the presence of evil in educational leadership may strike some as "overreaching" or "over-reacting" to some historic schooling dilemmas, it may be more apt than at first believed. What are we to make of educational leadership practices that embrace continuing forms of repression and social injustice in the schools? Is it merely incompetence or ignorance, or is it evil or even malignant?

Finally, what few researchers want to acknowledge is that their activities occur in what have been called "epistemic communities" (Usher and Edwards 1996, 149). The implication is the following:

> This location of research means that any piece of research always carries within itself an epistemology—a theory about knowledge and truth and their relationship to the world of "reality." This epistemology is never "innocent" because it always contains within itself a set of values—which means that there is always a *politics* of research, an implication of research within power relations. (149)

The truth is that "research is a practice of knowing that constructs a reality to know about". In other words, research is a kind of painting.

5. THE CONTINUED SLIDE TOWARD MARKETIZATION AND FOR-PROFIT METAPHORS IN PREPARATION PROGRAMS REMOVES THE MORAL IMPERATIVE TO IMPROVE THE COMMON GOOD IN SOCIETY. THIS TREND IS PROFOUNDLY ANTIDEMOCRATIC.

Recently our field has been attacked for a number of alleged failures. Those assaults have ranged from conservative think tanks who speak to the false necessity of having a "license to lead" and who proffer that the pipeline is "faulty" (Broad Foundation and Thomas B. Fordham Institute 2003) and that by "opening up" the field to ex-business executives, generals, and admirals, the impact will be salutary. We have even been advised to drop the Ed.D. degree and look toward business schools and the MBA as the model to adopt (Levine 2005). This recommendation flies in the face of the fact that current business leaders have considerably less confidence placed in them from the general public than educational leaders (Brush 2006). In fact, in the second annual poll on leadership conducted for *U.S. News and World Report* and Harvard University's Center for Public Leadership, "eighty-three percent of Americans say corporate leaders are more concerned with the bottom line than running their companies well" (Brush 2006, 56).

What is at stake in these attacks on our preparation programs is the concept of the educational leader as one promoting the common good, that is, the idea of *civic humanism*. K. S. Emery and Ohanian (2004) call this attack, sponsored by such organizations as the Business Round Table, part of the "hijacking of American education" (1), and J. R. Wiens reflected similarly:

> It dawned on us that the language of reform was not primarily and centrally about education. Rather, it was about economic ideology, sometimes called "the business agenda"—full of phrases like economic advantage, competition, customer satisfaction, consumers, products, stakeholders, entrepreneurship, human resources, and the like. . . . The words of educational reform revealed its purposes, leaving us feeling betrayed. Second, any serious notions of education seemed absent from the debate—indeed, the discussion sounded to us like the promotion of a kind of economic patriotism (our country and its people will lose their "competitive advantage"). (2006, 216)

Preparation programs for public education leaders should consider how the purposes of public education to promote the common good can and are being subverted by an ideology of profit and privatization and rededicate themselves to preparing educational leaders devoted to "the spirit of the commonweal that has always been the central expectation of public education" (Houston 2006, 5).

Graduates of our preparation programs should become critical observers of laws and proposals that frame educational problems within "for-profit" models. Students and parents are not customers. Teachers are not workers and educational leaders are not corporate CEOs. Our graduates should be thoroughly schooled in the discourse and linguistic phraseology of what Emery and Ohanian call "ed-bizspeak" (2004, 13) so that the terms can be deconstructed and unmasked for the true values they represent.

We have a choice to make on how we shape the purposes and content of graduate education. My belief is that we should reframe and rededicate the work of the doctor of education to focus on practices which will lead to a more just society, and the research which comes to define that degree will "uncover and document what is happening from the perspective of those being ill served to publicize inequities in the existing system and advocate for the victims of the system" (Riehl and Firestone 2005, 160). Our clarity on what we stand for is crucial not only to our success but to the long-term future of our profession and the schools, which should be instruments of creating a more just society.

Appendix

These articles published in *Educational Administration Quarterly* in the time period 2004–2006 met four or more of R. H. Brown's (1977) criteria for content which could be called *cognitive aesthetics.*

Year	Month	Author(s)	Title	Method	Total Cognitive Aesthetics Criteria Met
2004	April	Robert J. Starratt	*The Dialogue of Scholarship*	Critical reflection	4
2005	August	Dana L. Mitra	*Adults Advising Youth: Leading While Getting Out of the Way*	Qualitative	4
2005	October	Mark A. Gooden	*The Role of an African American Principal in an Urban Information Technology High School*	Qualitative	4
2005	October	Michael E. Dantley	*African American Spirituality and Cornel West's Notions of Prophetic Pragmatism: Restructuring Educational Leadership in American Urban Schools*	Conceptual/ critical reflection	4
2005	February	Mengli Song and Cecil G. Miskel	*Who are the Influentials? A Cross-State Social Network Analysis of the Reading Policy Domain*	Quantitative/ qualitative	4

(*continued*)

Year	Month	Author(s)	Title	Method	Total Cognitive Aesthetics Criteria Met
2005	February	Edith A. Rusch	*Institutional Barriers to Organizational Learning in School Systems: The Power of Silence*	Qualitative	4
2005	April	Lois Andre-Bechely	*Public School Choice at the Intersection of Voluntary Integration and Not-So-Good Neighborhood Schools: Lessons from Parents' Experiences*	Qualitative	5
2005	December	Tondra L. Loder	*Women Administrators Negotiate Work-Family Conflicts in Changing Times: An Intergenerational Perspective*	Qualitative	4
2006	February	Dean Fink and Carol Brayman	*School Leadership Succession and the Challenges of Change*	Qualitative	4
2006	December	Kathleen M. Brown	*Leadership for Social Justice and Equity: Evaluating a Transformative Framework and Andragogy*	Quantitative/ qualitative	4

Source: R. H. Brown (1977). *A Poetic for Sociology.* Cambridge, UK: Cambridge University Press.

References

Ackerman, R., and P. Maslin-Ostrowski. (2002). *The wounded leader: How real leadership emerges in times of crisis.* San Francisco: Jossey-Bass.

Aczel, A. (1996). *Fermat's last theorem: Unlocking the secret of the ancient mathematical problem.* New York: Four Walls Eight Windows.

Alston, J. A. (2005, Fall). Answering the call: Democracy, leadership, and the challenge of social justice. *UCEA Review* 42 (3): 16–17.

Anderson, G. (2001, July–September). Disciplining leaders: A critical discourse analysis of the ISLLC national examination and performance standards in educational administration. *International Journal of Leadership in Education* 4 (3): 199–216.

Argyris, C. (1972). *The applicability of organizational sociology.* Cambridge, MA: Harvard University Press.

Atkinson, P. (1990). *The ethnographic imagination: Textual constructions of reality.* London: Routledge.

Attenborough, R., ed. (1982). *The words of Gandhi.* New York: Newmarket Press.

Ball, P. (2006). *The devil's doctor: Paracelsus and the world of renaissance magic and science.* New York: Farrar, Straus, and Giroux.

Beck, L. (1994). *Reclaiming educational administration as a caring profession.* New York: Teachers College Press.

Beck, L., and W. Foster. (1999). Administration and community: Considering challenges, exploring possibilities. In J. Murphy and K. S. Louis, eds., *Handbook of research on educational administration,* 337–58. San Francisco: Jossey-Bass.

Bell, T. H. (1988). *The thirteenth man: A Reagan cabinet memoir.* New York: Free Press.

Beveridge, W. I. B. (1950). *The art of scientific investigation.* New York: Vintage Books.

Blasé, J., and J. Blasé. (2003). *Breaking the silence: Overcoming the problem of principal mistreatment of teachers.* Thousand Oaks, CA: Corwin Press.

Blount, J. (1998). *Destined to rule the schools: Women and the superintendency, 1873–1995.* Albany: State University of New York Press.

———. (2005). *Fit to teach: Same-sex desire, gender, and school work in the twentieth century.* Albany: State University of New York Press.

Boas, G. (1984). Ideology. In D. Runes, ed., *Dictionary of philosophy,* 156. Totowa, NJ: Rowman & Allanheld.

Bottery, M. (2004). *The challenges of educational leadership: Values in a globalized age.* London: Paul Chapman.

Boudin, R. (1989). *The analysis of ideology.* Chicago: University of Chicago Press.

Boyan, N. J., ed. (1988). *Handbook of research on educational administration.* New York: Longmans.

Broad Foundation and Thomas B. Fordham Institute (2003). *Better leaders for America's schools: A manifesto.* Retrieved February 11, 2004, from www.edexcellence.net/doc/Manifesto.pdf.

Brooks, J. S. (2006). *The dark side of school reform: Teaching in the space between reality and utopia.* Lanham, MD: Rowman & Littlefield Education.

Brown, F. (2005, October). African Americans and school leadership: An introduction. *Educational Administration Quarterly* 41 (4): 585–90.

Brown, K. M. (2006, Summer). A transformative andragogy for principal preparation programs. *UCEA Review* 45 (2): 1–5.

Brown, R. H. (1977). *A poetic for sociology.* Cambridge: Cambridge University Press.

Brush, S. (2006, October 30). A vote of no confidence. *U.S. News & World Report,* 56.

Callahan, R. E. (1962). *Education and the cult of efficiency.* Chicago: University of Chicago Press.

Capper, C. A. (1999, June-July). (Homo)sexualities, organizations, and administration: Possibilities for in(queer)y. *Educational Researcher* 28 (5): 4–11.

Canguilhem, G. (1988). *Ideology and rationality in the history of the life sciences.* Trans. A. Goldhammer. Cambridge, MA: MIT Press.

Carlyle, T. (1935). *On heroes, hero-worship, and the hero in history.* London: Oxford University Press.

Cartier-Bresson, H. (2005). *The mind's eye.* New York: Aperture.

Cassirer, E. (1956). *An essay on man.* Garden City, NY: Doubleday.

Cibulka, J. (2004, Spring). The case for academic program standards in educational administration: Toward a mature profession. *UCEA Review* 46 (2): 1–4.

Clifford, J. (1986). On ethnographic allegory. In J. Clifford & G. E. Marcus, eds., *Writing culture: The poetics and politics of ethnography.* Berkeley: University of California Press.

Cook, K. S. (1977). Exchange and power in networks of interorganizational relations. *Sociological Quarterly* 18: 62–82.

Crow, G. M. (2006, Winter). Democracy and educational work in an age of complexity. *UCEA Review* 43 (1): 1–5.

Crow, G., C. Hausman, and J. P. Scribner. (2002). Reshaping the role of the school principal. In J. Murphy, ed., *The educational leadership challenge: Redefining leadership for the twenty-first century*, 189–210. Chicago: University of Chicago Press.

Cuban, L. (1976). *Urban school chiefs under fire.* Chicago: University of Chicago Press.

———. (2004). *The blackboard and the bottom line: Why schools can't be businesses.* Cambridge: Harvard University Press.

Cunningham, W., and P. Cordeiro. (2000). *Educational administration: A problem-based approach.* Boston: Allyn & Bacon.

Dantley, M. (2005, October). African American spirituality and Cornel West's notions of prophetic pragmatism: Restructuring educational leadership in American urban schools. *Educational Administration Quarterly* 41 (4): 651–74.

Deal, T. E., and K. D. Peterson. (1994). *The leadership paradox: Balancing logic and artistry in schools.* San Francisco: Jossey-Bass.

Derrida, J. (1987). *The truth in painting.* Trans. G. Bennington and I. McLeod. Chicago: University of Chicago Press.

Dewey, J. (1929). *The sources of a science of education.* New York: Horace Liveright.

———. (1958/1934). *Art as experience.* New York: G. P. Putnam's Sons.

———. (1964/1926). Affective thought in logic and painting. In R. Archambault, ed., *John Dewey on education: Selected writings,* 141–48). New York: Modern Library.

Duffy, J. (1979). *The healers: A history of American medicine.* Urbana: University of Illinois Press.

Duke, D. L. (1989). The aesthetics of leadership. In J. L. Burdin, ed., *School leadership: A contemporary reader,* 345–65. Newbury Park, CA: Sage.

Dunham, B. (1964). *Heroes and heretics: A social history of dissent.* New York: Alfred A. Knopf.

Dyson, M. E. (2004). We were never what we used to be: Black youth, pop culture, and the politics of nostalgia. In M. E. Dyson, *The Michael Eric Dyson reader,* 418–42. New York: Basic Civitas Books.

Emery, K., and S. Ohanian. (2004). *Why is corporate America bashing our public schools?* Portsmouth, NH: Heinemann.

English, F. (2000, April–June). Psssst! What does one call a set of non-empirical beliefs required to be accepted on faith and enforced by authority? [Answer: a religion, aka the ISLLC standards]. *International Journal of Leadership in Education* 3 (2): 151–58.

———. (2001, January–March). What paradigm shift? An interrogation of Kuhn's idea of normalcy in the research practice of educational administration. *International Journal of Leadership in Education* 4 (1): 29–38.

———. (2002, March). The point of scientificity, the fall of the epistemological dominos, and the end of the field of educational administration. *Studies in Philosophy and Education* 21 (2): 109–36.

———. (2003a, March). Cookie-cutter leaders for cookie-cutter schools: The teleology of standardization and the de-legitimization of the university in educational leadership preparation. *Leadership and Policy in Schools* 2 (1): 27–46.

———. (2003b). Tsar khorosh, boyary polkhi—The ISLLC standards and the enshrinement of mystical authoritarianism as anti-change doctrine in educational leadership preparation programs. In F. Lunenburg and C. Carr, eds., *Shaping the future: Policy, partnerships, and emerging perspectives,* 112–33. Lanham, MD: Scarecrow Press.

———. (2004, Spring). Undoing the "done deal": Reductionism, ahistoricity, and pseudo-science in the knowledge base and standards for educational administration. *UCEA Review* 46 (2): 5–7.

———. (2005). Introduction: A metadiscursive perspective on the landscape of educational leadership in the twenty-first century. In F. English, ed., *The SAGE handbook of educational leadership: Advances in theory, research, and practice,* ix–xvi. Thousand Oaks, CA: SAGE.

———. (2006a, August). Understanding leadership in education: Life writing and its possibilities. *Journal of Educational Administration and History* 38 (2): 141–54.

———. (2006b, August). The unintended consequences of a standardized knowledge base in advancing educational leadership preparation. *Educational Administration Quarterly* 42 (3): 461–72.

———. (2007). *The NRC's scientific research in education: It isn't even wrong.* In F. English and G. Furman, eds., *Research and educational leadership: Navigating the new national research council guidelines,* 1–38. Lanham, MD: Rowman & Littlefield Education.

———. (2008). *Educational leadership as a performing art.* Thousand Oaks, CA: SAGE.

English, F., and G. Furman, eds. (2007). *Research and educational leadership: Navigating the new national research council guidelines.* Lanham, MD: Rowman & Littlefield Education.

Erdmann, K. (2005). Like everyone else. In K. M. Takakuwa, N. Rubashkin, and K. E. Herzig, eds., *What I learned in medical school: Personal stories of young doctors,* 168–76. Berkeley: University of California Press.

Fazzaro, C., J. Walter, and K. McKerrow. (1995). Educational administration in a postmodern society: Implications for moral practice. In S. J. Maxcy, ed., *Postmodern school leadership: Meeting the crisis in educational administration,* 85–96. Westport, CT: Praeger.

Feyerabend, P. (1993). *Against method.* London: Verso.

———. (1995). *Problems of empiricism.* Vol. 2. Cambridge: Cambridge University Press.

———. (1996). *Farewell to reason.* London: Verso.

Foucault, M. (1974). *The archaeology of knowledge.* London: Tavistock.

Furman, G., and C. Shields. (2005). How can educational leaders promote and support social justice and democratic community in schools? In W. A. Firestone and C. Riehl, eds., *A new agenda for research in educational leadership,* 119–37. New York: Teachers College Press.

Furman, G., and R. Starratt. (2002). Leadership for democratic community in schools. In J. Murphy, ed., *The educational leadership challenge: Redefining leadership for the twenty-first century,* 105–33. Chicago: University of Chicago Press.

Gadamer, H. G. (1977). *Philosophical hermeneutics.* Trans. D. E. Linge. Berkeley: University of California Press.

———. (1983). *Reason in the age of science.* Trans. F. G. Lawrence. Cambridge, MA: MIT Press.

Gandhi, M. (1968/1927). *An autobiography or the story of my experiments with truth. Book 2.* Trans. M. Desai. Ahmedabad: Navajuivan Press.

Giddens, A. (1984). *The continuation of society.* Berkeley: University of California Press.

Glickman, C., S. Gordon, and Ross-Gordon. (2007). *Supervision and instructional leadership: A developmental approach.* Boston: Pearson.

Goodall, H. L., Jr. (2000). *Writing the new ethnography.* Walnut Creek, CA: AltaMira Press.

Gordon, R. (1993). *The alarming history of medicine.* New York: St. Martin's Griffin.

Gratzer, W. (2002). *Eurekas and euphorias: The Oxford book of scientific anecdotes.* Oxford: Oxford University Press.

Greenfield, T. B., and P. Ribbins. (1993). *Greenfield on educational administration: Towards a humane science.* New York: Routledge.

Haack, S. (1996). *Evidence and inquiry: Towards reconstruction in epistemology.* Oxford: Blackwell.

Habermas, J. (1991). *On the logic of the social sciences.* Trans. S. W. Nicholsen and J. A. Stark. Cambridge, MA: MIT Press.

Haggard, H. W. (2004). *From medicine man to doctor: The story of the science of healing.* Mineola, NY: Dover.

Haller, E., and K. Strike. (1986). *An introduction to educational administration: Social, legal, and ethical perspectives.* New York: Longman.

Hanson, E. M. (1991). *Educational administration and organizational behavior.* Boston: Allyn & Bacon.

Heller, E. (1988). *The importance of Nietzsche: Ten essays.* Chicago: University of Chicago Press.

Hess, F. M. (2003). *A license to lead? A new leadership agenda for America's schools.* Washington, DC: Progressive Policy Institute.

Hessel, K., and J. Holloway. (2002). *A framework for school leaders: Linking the ISLLC standards to practice.* Princeton, NJ: Educational Testing Service.

Holman, L. (2005). Sometimes, all you can do is laugh. In K. Takakuwa, N. Rubashkin, and K. Herzig, eds., *What I learned in medical school: Personal stories of young doctors,* 114–20). Berkeley: University of California Press.

Honig, M. and Seashore Louis, K. (2007, February) A new agenda for research in educational leadership: A conversational review, 43, 1, 138–48.

House, E. R. (1998). *Schools for sale.* New York: Teachers College Press.

Houston, P. (2006). The superintendent: Championing the deepest purposes of education. In P. Kelleher and R. Van Der Bogert, eds., *Voices for democracy: Struggles and celebrations of transforming leaders*, 109. 105 Yearbook of the National Society for the Study of Education. Malden, MA: Blackwell.

Hoy, W., and C. Miskel. (1982). *Educational administration: Theory, research, and practice.* New York: Random House.

Iyer, R. (1973). *The moral and political thought of Mahatma Gandhi.* New York: Oxford University Press.

Johnson, P. (1996). Antipodes: Plato, Nietzsche, and the moral dimension of leadership. In P. S. Temes, ed., *Teaching leadership,* 13–44. New York: Peter Lang.

Keeton, M. (1984). Empiricism. In D. Runes, ed., *Dictionary of philosophy,* 104–5. Totowa, NJ: Rowman & Allanheld.

Kellerman, B. (2004). *Bad leadership.* Boston: Harvard Business School Press.

Kieran, M. (2005). *Revealing art.* London: Routledge.

Klass, P. (1987). *A not entirely benign procedure: Four years as a medical student.* New York: Penguin.

Kochan, F., B. Jackson, and D. Duke. (1999). *A thousand voices from the fire line: A study of educational leaders, their jobs, their preparation, and the problems they face.* Columbia, MO: UCEA.

Kuhn, T. S. (1996). *The structure of scientific revolutions.* Chicago: University of Chicago Press.

Lakatos, I. (1999) *The methodology of scientific research programmes.* Cambridge: Cambridge University Press.

Lakomski, G. (2005). *Managing without leadership: Towards a theory of organizational functioning.* Amsterdam: Elsevier.

Lantham, A., and J. Holloway. (1999, December). The profession of school superintendent: An analysis of the responsibilities and knowledge areas important for beginning school superintendents. Princeton, NJ: Educational Testing Service.

Larson, C., and K. Murtadha. (2002). Leadership for social justice. In J. Murphy, ed., *The educational leadership challenge: Redefining lead-*

ership for the twenty-first century, 134–61. Chicago: University of Chicago Press.

Lawrence-Lightfoot, S. (1983). *The good high school: Portraits of character and culture.* New York: Basic Books.

Lawrence-Lightfoot, S., and J. Hoffman Davis. (1997). *The art and science of portraiture.* San Francisco: Jossey-Bass.

LeFanu, J. (1999). *The rise and fall of modern medicine.* New York: Carroll & Graf.

Levin, H. M. (2006, November). Can research improve educational leadership? *Educational Researcher* 35 (8): 38–43.

Levine, A. (2005). *Educating school leaders.* Washington, D.C. The Education Schools Project.

Lewontin, R. C. (1991). *Biology as ideology: The doctrine of DNA.* New York: HarperCollins.

Lugg, C. (2003). Sissies, faggots, lezzies, and dykes: Gender, sexual orientation, and a new politics of education? *Educational Administration Quarterly* 39 (1): 95–134.

Lugg, C., and J. W. Koschoreck, eds. (2003). The final closet [Special Issue], *Journal of School Leadership* 13 (1).

Lunenburg, F., and A. Ornstein. (1991). *Educational administration: Concepts and practices.* Belmont, CA: Wadsworth.

Mahitivanichcha, K., and A. Rorrer. (2006, October). Women's choices within market constraints: Re-visioning access to and participation in the superintendency. *Educational Administration Quarterly* 42 (4): 483–517.

Mann, M. (2003). *The sources of social power.* Cambridge: Cambridge University Press.

Marshall, C., and M. Oliva. (2006). *Leadership for social justice: Making revolutions in education.* Boston: Pearson.

Maxcy, S. J. (1991). *Educational leadership: A critical pragmatic perspective.* New York: Bergin & Garvey.

——. (1994). Afterwords: Postmodern directions in educational leadership. In S. J. Maxcy, ed., *Postmodern school leadership: Meeting the crisis in educational administration,* 153–62. Westport, CT: Praeger.

Merriam-Webster. (2003). *Merriam Webster's collegiate dictionary.* Springfield, MA: Merriam-Webster.

Monahan, T. (2005). *Globalization, technological change, and public education.* New York: Routledge.

Motterlini, M., ed. (1999). *For and against method: Imre Lakatos and Paul Feyerabend*. Chicago: University of Chicago Press.

Murphy, J. (1999). *The quest for a center: Notes on the state of the profession of educational leadership*. Columbia, MO: UCEA.

———. (2000, October–December). A response to English. *International Journal of Leadership in Education* 3 (4): 399–410.

———. (2002). Reculturing the profession of educational leadership: New blueprints. In J. Murphy, ed., *The educational leadership challenge: Redefining leadership for the twenty-first century*, 65–82. Chicago: University of Chicago Press.

———. (2005). Unpacking the foundations of ISLLC standards and addressing concerns in the academic community. *Educational Administration Quarterly* 41 (1): 154–91.

Murphy, J., and W. Hawley. (2003, Fall). The AASA "leadership for learning" masters program. *TEA-SIG* (Teaching in Educational Administration) 10 (2): 1–6.

Murphy, J., and K. Seashore Louis, eds. (1999). *Handbook of research on educational administration*. 2nd ed. San Francisco: Jossey-Bass.

Murphy, J., J. Yff, and N. Shipman. (2000, January-March). Implementation of the interstate school leaders licensure consortium standards. *International Journal of Leadership in Education* 3 (1): 17–40.

Murtadha, K., and D. M. Watts. (2005, October). Linking the struggle for education and social justice: Historical perspectives of African-American leadership in schools. *Educational Administration Quarterly* 41 (4): 591–608.

National Research Council. (2002). *Scientific research in education*. Ed. R. J. Shavelson and L. Towne. Washington, DC: National Academy Press.

Nicholaides, N., and A. Gaynor. (1989). *Notes on reform*. Charlottesville, VA: NPBEA.

Nielsen, J. S. (2004). *The myth of leadership: Creating leaderless organizations*. Palo Alto, CA: Davies-Black.

Nuland, S. B. (1988). *Doctors: The biography of medicine*. New York: Alfred A. Knopf.

———. (2003). *The doctors' plague: Germs, childbed fever, and the strange story of Ignac Semmelweis*. New York: W. W. Norton.

Ortiz, F. I., and C. Marshall. (1988). Women in educational administration. In N. J. Boyan, ed., *Handbook of research on educational administration*, 123–42. New York: Longmans.

Owen, R. (1987). *Organizational behavior in education.* Englewood Cliffs, NJ: Prentice-Hall.

Peirce, C. S. (1955). *Philosophical writings of Peirce.* Ed. J. Buchler. New York: Dover.

Perutz, M. (1995, December 21). The pioneer defended. *New York Review of Books,* 42 (20): 54–58.

Peters, B. G. (1999). *Institutional theory in political science: The "new institutionalism."* New York: Continuum.

Popper, K. R. (1968). *The logic of scientific discovery.* New York: Harper & Row.

Porter, R. (1999). *The greatest benefit to mankind: A medical history of humanity.* New York: W. W. Norton.

———. (2003). *Flesh in the age of reason.* New York: W. W. Norton.

Pounder, D., and R. Johnson. (2007, February 13). University of Utah's interest in renewing EAQ contract for 3 year period—July 1, 2007 through June 30, 2010. Unpublished memo to M. Young, C. Lugg, and UCEA Executive Committee.

Price, L. (1999). Leontyne Price. In B. Lanker, ed., *I dream a world: Portraits of black women who changed America,* 48–49. New York: Stewart, Tabori & Chang.

Riehl, C., and W. A. Firestone. (2005). What research methods should be used to study educational leadership? In W. A. Firestone and C. Riehl, eds., *A new agenda for research in educational leadership,* 156–70. New York: Teachers College Press.

Rorrer, A. (2002, Fall). Educational leadership and institutional capacity for equity. *UCEA Review* 43 (3): 1–5.

Rosenbaum, R. (1998). *Explaining Hitler. The search for the origins of his evil.* New York: Random House.

Rost, J. (1991). *Leadership for the twenty-first century.* New York, CT: Praeger.

Rousmaniere, K. (2005). *Citizen teacher: The life and leadership of Margaret Haley.* Albany: State University of New York Press.

Rusch, E. A. (2005, February). Institutional barriers to organizational learning in school systems: The power of silence. *Educational Administration Quarterly* 41 (1): 83–120.

Saltman, K. J. (2000). *Collateral Damage: Corporatizing public schools: A threat to democracy.* Lanham, MD: Rowman & Littlefield.

Samier, E. A. (2007a). Canadian federal mandarin memoirs: On the formation of the public service ethos. *Zeitschrift fur Kanada-Studien* 48 (1): 103–19.

———. (2007b). The shadow side of compassion: Exploring covert practices of secrecy and tradecraft in educational administration. Unpublished paper proposal.

Samier, E. A., and A. Stanley. (2006). The art and legacy of the romantic tradition: Implications for power, self-determination, and administration. In E. A. Samier and R. J. Bates, eds., *Aesthetic dimensions of educational administration and leadership,* 34–44. London: Routledge.

Samier, E. A., R. J. Bates, and A. Stanley. (2006). Foundations and history of the social aesthetic. In E. A. Samier and R. J. Bates, eds., *Aesthetic dimensions of educational administration and leadership,* 3–18. London: Routledge.

Schama, S. (2006). *The power of art.* New York: HarperCollins.

Schmolders, C. (2000). *Hitler's face: The biography of an image.* Trans. A. Daub. Philadelphia: University of Pennsylvania Press.

Sears, J. T. (1993). Responding to sexual diversity of faculty and students: Sexual praxis and the critically reflective administrator. In C. A. Capper, ed., *Educational administration in a pluralistic society,* 110–72. Albany: State University of New York Press.

Seashore Louis, K., and M. Honig. (2007, February). A new agenda for research in educational leadership: A conversational review. *Educational Administration Quarterly* 43 (1): 138–48.

Shakeshaft, C. (1999). The struggle to create a more gender-inclusive profession. In J. Murphy and K. S. Louis, eds., *Handbook of research on educational administration*, 2nd ed., 99–118. San Francisco: Jossey-Bass.

Shipman, N. J., J. A. Queen, and H. A. Peel. (2007). *Transforming school leadership with ISLLC and ELCC.* Larchmont, NY: Eye on Education.

Shoho, A., B. Merchant, and C. Lugg. (2005). Social justice: Seeking a common language. In F. English, ed., *The SAGE handbook of educational leadership: Advances in theory, research, and practice,* 47–67. Thousand Oaks, CA: SAGE.

Smircich, L. (1983). Concepts of culture and organizational analysis. *Administrative Science Quarterly* 28: 81–104.

Smith, L. G., and J. Smith. (1994). *Lives in education: A narrative of people and ideas.* New York: St. Martin's Press.

Song, M., and C. G. Miskel. (2005, February). Who are the influentials? A cross-state social network analysis of the reading policy domain. *Educational Administration Quarterly* 41 (1): 7–48.

Speer, A. (1970). *Inside the third reich: Memoirs.* Trans. R. and C. Winston. New York: Macmillan.

Spillane, J. (2006). *Distributed leadership.* San Francisco: Jossey-Bass.

Starratt, R. J. (1993). *The drama of leadership.* London: Falmer Press.

Stein, M. K., and J. Spillane. (2005). What can researchers on educational leadership learn from research on teaching? Building a bridge. In W. A. Firestone and C. Rhiel, eds., *A new agenda for research in educational leadership,* 28–45. New York: Teachers College Press.

Sterba, J. (1999). Ideology. In R. Audi, ed., *The Cambridge dictionary of philosophy,* 2nd ed., 416. Cambridge: Cambridge University Press.

Takakuwa, K. M., N. Rubashkin, and K. E. Herzig, eds. (2005). *What I learned in medical school: Personal stories of young doctors.* Berkeley: University of California Press.

Tannenbaum, R. J. (1996). The profession of school administrator: An analysis of the responsibilities and knowledge areas important for beginning school administration. Princeton, NJ: Educational Testing Service.

———. (1997). Content validation of the interstate school leaders licensure consortium school leaders licensure assessment. Princeton, NJ. Educational Testing Service.

Tillman, L. C. (2002). Culturally sensitive research approaches: An African American perspective. *Educational Researcher* 31 (9): 3–12.

———. (2003). From rhetoric to reality? Educational administration and the lack of racial and ethnic diversity within the profession. *UCEA Review* 45 (3): 1–4.

Usher, R., and R. Edwards. (1996). *Postmodernism and education.* London: Routledge.

Watt, J. (1994). *Ideology, objectivity, and education.* New York: Teachers College Press.

Weiner, E. J. (2005). *Private learning, public needs: The neoliberal assault on democratic education.* New York: Peter Lang.

Wellman, F. L. (1962). *The art of cross-examination.* New York: Collier.

West, C. (1999). Race and modernity. In Cornel West, *The Cornel West reader,* 55–86. New York: Basic Civitas Books.

Wiens, J. R. (2006). Educational leadership as civic humanism. In P. Kelleher and R. Van Der Bogert, eds., *Voices for democracy: Struggles and celebrations of transforming leaders,* 199–225. Malden, MA: Blackwell.

Wolcott, H. F. (1973). *The man in the principal's office: An Ethnography.* New York: Holt, Rinehart & Winston.

———. (1995). *The art of fieldwork.* Walnut Creek, CA: AltaMira Press.

———. (1999). *Ethnography: a way of seeing.* Walnut Creek, CA: AltaMira Press.

Wood, A. (1995). Russell's philosophy: A study of its development. In B. Russell, *My philosophical development,* 189–205. London: Routledge.

Young, M. D., and G. R. Lopez. (2005). The nature of inquiry in educational leadership. In F. English, ed., *The SAGE handbook of educational leadership,* 337–61. Thousand Oaks, CA: SAGE.

Index

About the Author

Fenwick W. English is the *R. Wendell Eaves Senior Distinguished Professor of Educational Leadership* in the School of Education at the University of North Carolina at Chapel Hill. He has been both a practitioner and a professor and served in leadership positions in K–12 education and higher education since 1961. Dr. English served as a middle-school principal in California, a project director in Arizona, an assistant superintendent in Florida, and a superintendent of schools in New York. In higher education he has served as a department chair, program coordinator, dean, and vice-chancellor of academic affairs. He has not only written about leadership in education, but he has been an educational leader in the public and private sectors. He was the elementary/secondary education practice director for KPMG Peat Marwick in the firm's Washington, D.C., office for three years and an associate executive director of the American Association of School Administrators (AASA). He is the author or coauthor of more than twenty-five books in education and also served as the general editor of the 2005 *SAGE Handbook of Educational Leadership* and the 2006 *SAGE Encyclopedia of Educational Leadership and Administration.* He was an author and coeditor (with Gail Furman) of the 2007 text *Research and Educational Leadership,* released by Rowman & Littlefield Education.

He has been a symposium presenter at Divisions A and L of the American Education Research Association, the University Council for Educational Administration (UCEA), and the National Council of Professors of Educational Administration (NCPEA), as well as BELMAS (British Educational Leadership Management Administration Society). He has been a member of the UCEA executive

committee since 2001 and was elected president of the University
Council for Educational Administration for 2006–2007. He has been
a professor in educational leadership programs at Lehigh University,
University of Cincinnati, University of Kentucky, Indiana–Purdue
University Fort Wayne, Iowa State University, and, since 2001, at
the University of North Carolina at Chapel Hill. He earned his B.S.
and M.S. from the University of Southern California, and his Ph.D.
from Arizona State University.